着物と日本の色

Kimono and the Colors of Japan

Kimono Collection of Katsumi Yumioka

着物には日本人の感性を凝縮した世界がある

私はもともと雑誌や TV コマーシャルなどのヘアー＆メイクを本業としていました。そういった中で、クリスチャン・ディオールのショーに参加したことはとても衝撃でした。日本にはない色使いと柄。デザイン、縫製。オートクチュールの素晴らしさに感動しました。一方で、着物の着付けもできましたので年齢を重ねるにしたがって、着物のスタイリングに関する仕事も増えその魅力にも目覚めていきました。着物にはどんなオートクチュールにも劣らない色と感性がありとても新鮮に映りました。中でも、大正時代の着物には西欧の文化にも通じる色や柄があることも知り、ついには着物のコレクションを始めることとなり、結果、壱の蔵というアンティーク着物ショップを持つことになりました。

西欧の文化が日本にどっと入ってきた大正時代に、当時の日本人はやわらかい応用力とセンスで着物の中に取り込んできました。また、西欧的なことだけではなく日本画などのデザインも高度な染色技術や刺繍などを駆使して再現してきました。本書では江戸時代末期から現代までの着物や帯の中から、色を軸としてセレクトした物を紹介しています。結果、より日本的なラインナップになりましたが、着るということを前提とした着物ではなく、絵画やオブジェなどの美術品と同じようにグラフィカルな視点で捉えることによってまた新しい着物の世界が広がるのではないでしょうか。

上述のように、日本の色を着物や帯の中に表現された色で分類した本書ですが、そもそも着物や帯には色々な色や柄が複合されてその世界が形成されているものです。ですから、単色を取り上げるには難しい部分もあります。その中で、日本人が生活の中で表現している私のイメージとしての日本の心の色を考えて分類しています。

喜びを表す場合に用いる白と赤と金。赤は太陽であり血、そして火。悲しみを表す場合には白と黒と銀。黒はすべてを被い尽くす闇であり悲しみ。黄色は収穫の喜びであり活力。待ち望んだ春の到来を桃色。畏敬の念は紫。大地の茶。木々の緑。空と海の青。

最後に、本書では紹介しきれなかった日本人の美的感覚、細部にまでわたる技術、季節感、そして、ユーモアセンスなどを又紹介できることを楽しみにしています。

弓岡勝美

Japanese Sensibilities Thrive in the World of Kimono

I started my career specializing in hair styling and make-up, during which I had the opportunity to participate in a Christian Dior show, which filled me with wonder and admiration. Dior's use of colors and patterns were nothing similar to what I had seen in Japan. For a long time that memory had an enormous influence on me. And as I fashioned my career toward becoming a kimono stylist, I soon realized that there was far more charm in the world of kimono colors than I had ever expected. I also noticed a similarity in the use of colors and patterns among western fashions and Taisho period kimono. Delighted by this alluring charm on a daily basis, I soon started collecting antique kimono, which led to the establishment of my antique kimono shop, *Ichinokura*.

It was during the Taisho period that western civilization and culture conquered Japanese society. Yet the Japanese people found a way to adapt their own kimono culture to include western influence. While integrating the western sense of style in to their own lifestyle, they found new dyeing and sewing techniques that enabled them to recreate traditional Japanese hues and designs. For this book, we have selected kimono and obi from the Edo period up to the present. Although we have selected pieces based on a color scheme, the result turned out to be a very traditional Japanese collection. We hope this presentation will show you another side of the kimono appeal - its pleasure and delight as a graphical art form.

Although we have attempted to categorize kimono and obi by color, the world of kimono is created by a combination of color and design and cannot be neatly divided according to a single formula. It is very difficult to describe the allure of kimono from only one aspect. Yet taking a look these combinations from one striking angle, we can discover the meanings and stories our ancestors tried to instill within the palette of the kimono.

We have organized the kimono and obi according to what I like to call "Japanese Kokoro no Iro" - colors of the Japanese heart. Each category presents an image of what Japanese people find individual colors to express or signify. For example, we use white, black and gold as an expression of cheer. Red indicates the sun, blood and fire. White, black and silver express sadness. Black communicates the poignant darkness that covers all things. Yellow is the joy of the harvest. Pink conveys the long awaited spring. Purple shows reverence. Brown articulates the land, green the trees, and blue the sky and sea.

There is so much more depth to the Japanese sense of beauty, our knowledge of technique, and our manners of expressing the seasons. I look forward to introducing such topics on another occasion.

Katsumi Yumioka

Kimono and the Colors of Japan
Kimono Collection of Katsumi Yumioka

Collection ©2005 Katsumi Yumioka
Published by PIE BOOKS

PIE BOOKS
2-32-4, Minami-Otsuka, Toshima-ku, Tokyo 170-005 Japan
Tel: +81-3-5395-4820 FAX: +81-3-5395-4821
e-mail: sales@piebooks.com
http://www.piebooks.com

ISBN978-4-89444-451-5 C0072
Printed in Japan

着 物 と 日 本 の 色

Kimono and the Colors of Japan

も く じ

Contents

赤 Red 11-27

	猩猩緋	しょうじょうひ	Poppy Red
朱色	しゅいろ	Scarlet
緋色	ひいろ	French Vermilion
真朱	しんしゅ	Cardinal
柿色	かきいろ	Persimmon Red
韓紅花	からくれない	Rose Red
蘇芳色	すおういろ	Raspberry Red
赤紅色	あかべにいろ	Geranium

緑 Green 39-55

萌葱色	もえぎいろ	Parrot Green
柳色	やなぎいろ	Mist Green
松葉色	まつばいろ	Jade Green
鶸色	ひわいろ	Light Lime Green
錆御納戸	さびおなんど	Blue Conifer
柳鼠	やなぎねずみ	Eggshell Green
木賊	とくさ	Spruce Green
青竹色	あおたけいろ	Jewel Green

桃 Pink 67-83

	珊瑚色	さんごいろ	Coral Pink
	中紅	なかべに	Cherry Pink
	鴇色	ときいろ	Cupid Pink
	躑躅色	つつじいろ	Azalea Pink
	桜色	さくらいろ	Very Pale Orchid Pink
	牡丹色	ぼたんいろ	Tree Peony Pink
	桃色	ももいろ	Fuchsia Pink
	薄紅	うすべに	Rose Pink

青 Blue 95-111

	花浅葱	はなあさぎ	Cerulean Blue
	縹色	はなだいろ	Sapphire Blue
	藍色	あいいろ	Marine Blue
	新橋色	しんばしいろ	Cyan Blue
	瑠璃色	るりいろ	Cobalt Blue
	浅葱色	あさぎいろ	Blue Turquoise
	紅掛空色	べにかけそらいろ	Salvia Blue
	瓶覗	かめのぞき	Horizon Blue

茶 Brown 123-139

	雀茶	すずめちゃ	Brick Red
	白茶	しらちゃ	Sand Beige
	栗皮茶	くりかわちゃ	Chestnut
	利休茶	りきゅうちゃ	Dusty Olive
	弁柄色	べんがらいろ	Copper Rust
	江戸茶	えどちゃ	Garnet Brown
	鳶色	とびいろ	Coconut Brown
	焦茶	こげちゃ	Van Dyke Brown

茶の組み合せ　Combination of Colors　140-149

紫 Purple 151-167

	牡丹	ぼたん	Fuchsia Purple
	深紫	こきむらさき	Deep Royal Purple
	紫紺	しこん	Blackish Purple
	紺	こん	Purple Navy
	似紫	にせむらさき	Plum
	桔梗色	ききょういろ	Violet
	黒紅	くろべに	Dusky Purple
	菖蒲色	しょうぶいろ	Iris

紫の組み合せ　Combination of Colors　168-177

赤

Red

太陽によって一日が明ける（アケ
ル）。そのアケルという言葉が「赤
＝アカ」になったとされる。太陽の
恵みである「陽」、暗闇の中でも
生活に光を与え安らぎをもたらす
「火」、体の中を流れる生命の根源
でもある「血」。これら赤色のもの
はすべて生きていくための根源を
なすものである。そのため人間に
とって赤色は神聖な色と言える。

It is with the sun that dawn breaks
each new day. As the Japanese word
for dawn and red are quite similar,
red has traditionally represented
the sun. The radiance that the sun
blesses us with brings light to even
the darkest life. The heat of red fire
brings us comfort. Blood, a deep
red, is also the foundation of life
that flows through the human body.
All these shades of red represent
the very basics of living. It is no
wonder that red is called "the
sacred color."

猩猩緋

Poppy Red

しょうじょうひ

黄味がかった鮮やかな朱色。中国の伝説に登場する、猿に似た霊獣「猩猩」の血で紅を染めたとされることにちなむ。室町時代末期にこの色で染められた毛織物の羅紗（らしゃ）が南蛮船で運ばれてきた。染料はサボテンに寄生するコチニール虫の雌から採取された赤色素。現在は「カルミン」と呼ばれ、化粧品や食品色素など広い用途で利用されている。

Shōjōhi: a vibrant vermilion with a touch of yellow. Poppy red is used to describe the bloodstained lips of the ape-like monster *Shōjō* that appears in a famous Chinese legend. At the end of the Muromachi period (1336-1573), thick woolen textiles dyed in poppy red were imported from Southeast Asia. The dye comes from the cochineal insect, a cacti-loving parasite. The modern name for this dye is carmine and is widely used in cosmetics and as food coloring.

朱色

Scarlet

しゅいろ

黄味を帯びた鮮明な赤色。朱色は縄文時代からあった最も古い色の一つで、貝塚などからこの色をあしらった土器や土偶なども見つかっている。土からつくる顔料としては朱が一番鮮やかなため、太陽や炎を示す色や権力を示す色として神事や祭事には欠かせないものだった。主成分は硫化水銀で、天然産のものは辰砂（しんしゃ）から精製される。

Shu-iro: a rich red tinted with yellow. Scarlet is one of the oldest colors, dating back to the prehistoric Jōmon period (10,000 B.C. – 300 B.C.) and often found on clay vessels and dolls discovered from ancient shell mounds. As this tinge was the most vibrant of the pigments extracted from earth, it was often used to represent the sun or fire, and as a symbol of authority in Shinto events and celebrations. The primary ingredient of the colorant is mercury sulfide, produced naturally by refining cinnabar.

15

緋色

French Vermilion

ひいろ

茜と灰汁（あく）で染めた強い黄味を帯びた赤色。飛鳥時代の孝徳天皇の冠位に見られる「真緋」、持統天皇の「緋（あけ）」や「浅緋（うすあけ）」も同色。色味が目立つことから武将が好んで用いた色でもあり、中でも武田軍の赤備（あかぞなえ）の軍団が有名。茜染めの技法は難しかったため江戸時代にはくちなしの黄で下染めし、その上に蘇芳で染められた「紅緋」が「緋」と呼ばれるようになった。

Hi-iro: a strong hue of red dyed with a blend of madder and lye. This color is dyed in the same manner as the deep vermilion seen in the crest of Emperor Kotoku or the two shades of vermilion in the crest of Emperor Jitō of the Asuka period (592-645). Military commanders favored this color for its striking tone, the Akazonae Corps of Takeda's Army was particularly well known for their use of French Vermilion. The difficulties of dyeing with madder were solved during the Edo period (1603-1867) by bottoming the material with yellow from the gardenia, then dyeing with rasberry red, resulting in the rich French.

真朱

Cardinal

しんしゅ

黒味の濃い赤色。真朱の「真」
は人工の「銀朱」に対して、自然
界の土の中から掘り出した硫化水
銀鉱物であることを示す。日本で
も縄文時代から発掘されており、
万葉集ではこの色が「まそほ」と
呼ばれている。また、一般的にこ
の真朱は「辰砂（しんしゃ）」と
呼ばれているが、これは中国湖南
省辰州で、朱の原料となる「朱砂
（しゅさ）」の良質なものが採れる
ことにちなんでいる。

Shinshu: a dark red tinged with
black. The Japanese word *shinshu*
is a combination of "pure" and
"cinnabar," indicating that this
color is created from the naturally
mined mercury sulfide, rather than
the man-made "silver cinnabar."
Mercury sulfide has been mined in
Japan since the Jōmon Period and
was referred to as *masoho* in the
classic, *Manyoshu* (*A Collection of
a Myriad Leaves*). Cardinal was also
known as *shinsha*, referring to the
location in Hunan Province, China,
where high quality cinnabar was
mined.

柿色

Persimmon Red

かきいろ

柿渋、紅柄で染めた、熟れた柿を思わせるにぶい黄赤で「柿渋色」を略したもの。歌舞伎で出てくる「柿色」は市川家の狂言でよく使われることから別名「団十郎茶」と言われる茶色で、この柿色とは別色。江戸前期の柿右衛門様式と言われる弁柄で絵付けをして焼いた陶磁器が「柿色」を代表する芸術品として知られている。

Kaki-iro: Dyed with the bitter juice of the persimmon and burnt ochre, the Japanese name was originally a lengthy "Persimmon tannin color" due to its resemblance to the dull yellow-red hue of ripe persimmons. The brownish tint *danjiro-cha*, often used in comic dramas by the Ichikawa Family of kabuki fame, goes by the same name but actually looks quite different. In the Kakiemon style of the early Edo period, pottery was decorated with burnt ochre and became known as the standard for persimmon red in the arts.

韓紅花

Rose Red

からくれない

紅花で染めた美しく濃い紅赤色。
エジプトやエチオピアからシルク
ロードを経由して日本に紅花が
渡ってきたのは5世紀ごろ。その
ときに「呉の国からやってきた染
料」という意味の「呉藍（くれあ
い）」が「紅（くれない）」となり、
平安時代に濃い紅花の赤色は「唐
紅、韓紅花」となったという説と、
「『から』は赤（やから）の略で紅
の鮮明な意味」という説がある。

Kara kurenai: a beautiful, rich rose
color dyed with safflower blossoms.
The safflower was introduced to
Japan from Egypt and Ethiopia in
about the fifth century via the Silk
Road. At that time, the dye was
called *kureai*, meaning "a dye from
the country of *Kure* (China)." But
the name was further adjusted into
the name *kurenai*, meaning rouge.
Apparently, the red created from
the rich tint of safflowers became
very popular in the Heian period
(794-1185), and the name was finally
tweaked into *karakurenai*, another
play on words meaning "bright red."

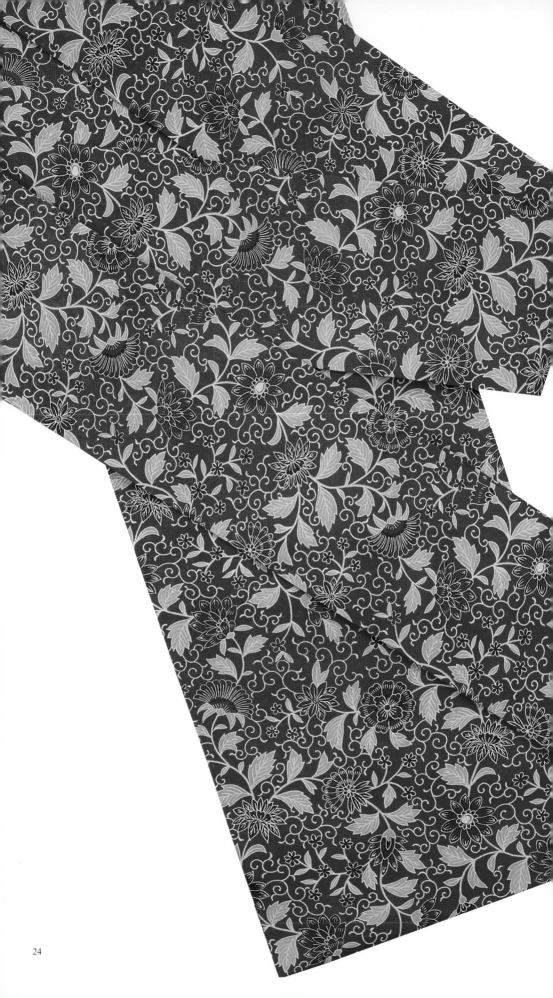

蘇芳色

Raspberry Red

すおういろ

青紫がかった暗赤色。マレー半島やインド南部に生育するマメ科のスオウの樹木の芯をせんじて染料とする。日本には奈良時代から薬材、染材として利用されてきた。古代の蘇芳染めは灰汁を使った紫がかった赤だったが、ミョウバンを使った鮮やかな赤、また鉄を使った黒みがかった赤にする染色法も用いられ、紅花や茜の代用としても用いられた。

Su'ou-iro: a dark shade of red highlighted with blue and purple. The wick of the leguminous sapanwood, native to the Malay Peninsula and southern part of India, is infused to create this rich dye. This ingredient has been used since the Nara Period as both a medicine and a dye. Ancient raspberry red dye was a purplish-red created with lye, but alum was also used to create a more vivid hue and iron was then added to bring in a black tint, both components serving as substitutes for safflower and madder.

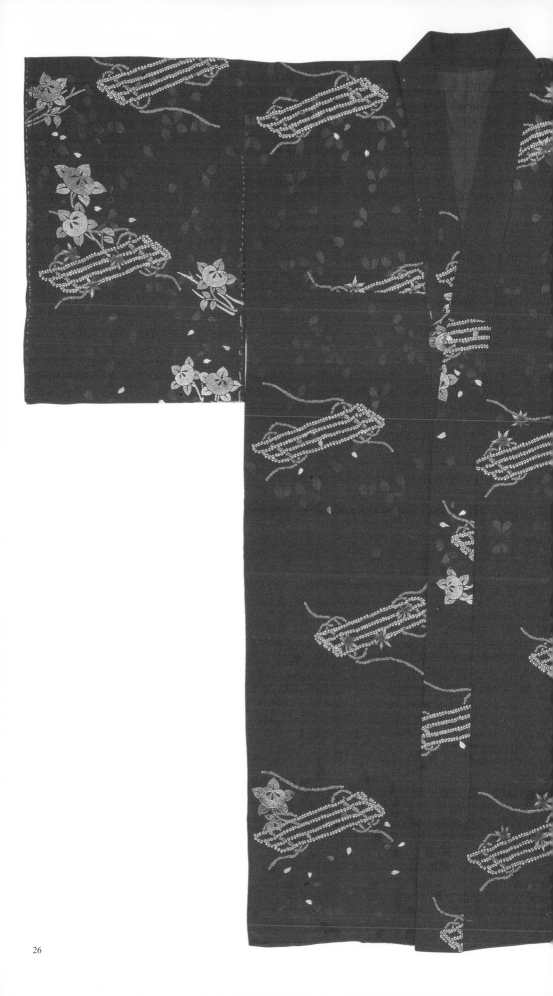

赤紅色

Geranium

あかべにいろ

鮮やかな冴えた紅赤色。江戸前
期から用いられてきた染色で、こ
の時代の京都の上流婦人が好む
小袖を記した書『御ひいなかた』
の小袖の地色にも見られる。赤や
紅が流行した貞享〜天保の時代
には、この赤紅で染めあげた鹿の
子染が大流行した。

Akabeni-iro: a vivid, dazzling red.
Used since the early part of the Edo
period, this color was mentioned as
a background color on the *kosode*
short-sleeved kimono described
in *Gohi' inakata*, a favorite picture
scroll among the upper-class ladies
in Kyoto. Of all the red and crimson
hues popular between the Jōkyō
and Tenpō eras (1684-1843), the
trendiest use of geranium was for
a dapple-dyed cloth resembling the
coat of a baby deer.

31

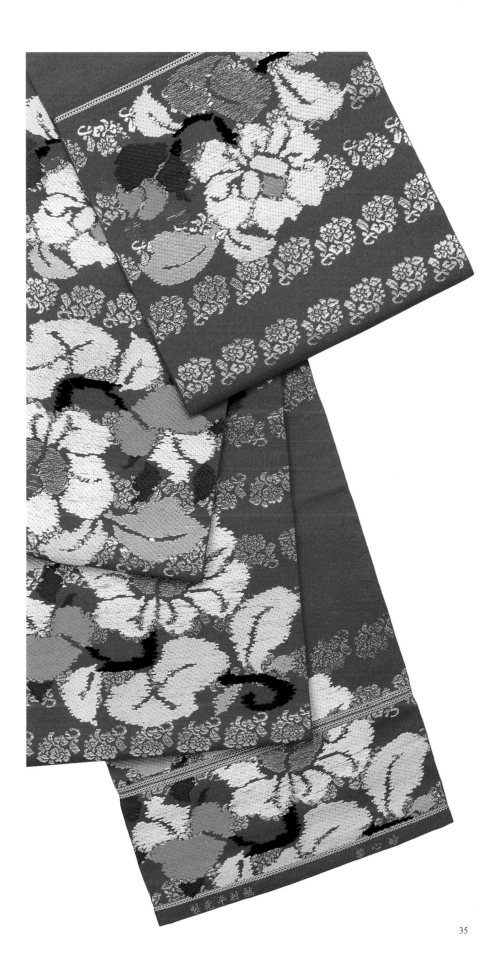

緑

Green

自然を象徴する「緑」。豊かな自
然のあるところであれば、どのよ
うな草木からも容易に色素を得
られるように思える。しかしなが
ら、草木の葉が持つ葉緑素とい
う色素は脆弱で、水に遭うとす
ぐに流れてしまう。単独で緑色
となる染料は世界中どこを探し
てもない。身近にいつもありなが
ら、たやすく再現することのでき
ない色である。

Green, the universal symbol of
nature. Where there is lush nature,
there is certain to be wonderful
coloring from any type of vegetation.
Yet, the chlorophyll that provides
the leaves their green pigment is
fragile and quickly washed away
when dampened. In fact, there is
no dye to be found throughout the
world that can alone create pure
green hues, a color so familiar yet
so difficult to recreate.

新緑が萌え出ずるような緑で、冴えた黄緑色。平安時代から用いられた色名で、青味がかった色を萌木、黄味がかった色を萌黄とも書かれる。色名の由来から特に若向きの色とされており、『平家物語』では斎藤実盛が老体とわからぬように萌葱縅（もえぎおどし）の鎧で出陣するくだりが書かれている。

Moegi-iro: a brilliant yellow-green like the flush of spring. The Japanese name, *moegi-iro*, dates back to the Heian period, and can be written with different characters to indicate a bluish or yellowish tone. The name itself indicates that this is a color for the younger set. In the *Tale of Heike*, it is written that Sanemori Saito hides the fact that he has aged by going into battle bearing a parrot-green suit of armor, signifying great power.

萌葱色

Parrot Green

もえぎいろ

やわらかい黄色がかった緑色で、
3月から4月にかけて柳の葉が萌
え出ずる時期の黄緑を表現して
いる。雅の人々は春風にそよぐは
かなげな柳をこよなく愛し、『万
葉集』や『源氏物語』など多く
の物語に登場する。また、萌葱
色の経糸（たていと）と白色の緯
糸（よこいと）で織った織物を指
すという文献もある。

Yanagi-iro: a soft yellow-green,
conveying the verdant hue we see
between March and April when
the willow tree buds appear. The
nobility especially loved the flitting,
fragile sight of the willow tree
blowing in a spring breeze, a popular
feature of many court stories such
as *Manyōshu* and *The Tale of Genji*.
Mist Green is often described in
literature for fabrics woven with
parrot green and white threads.

柳色

Mist Green

やなぎいろ

松葉色

Jade Green

まつばいろ

松の葉のような深みのある青緑色で、刈安と蓼藍を重ねて染めた。「松の葉色」とも言われ、『枕草子』には「狩衣は香染の薄き、白き、ふくさ、赤色、松の葉色…」とある。気候の変化に強く常に緑を保つ松は、不変や長寿のシンボルとして古来からあがめられ、この松葉色も生命力を示す色として愛用された。

Matsuba-iro: a blue-green with the deep hue of pinestraw, dyed alternately in eulalia (silver grass) and Chinese indigo. This shade is dubbed pinestraw green in *The Pillow Book* to describe the informal attire of the court nobility: "hunting wear was of sheer, bleached crepe material colored red and pinestraw green, and slightly scented." The pine tree has been a favorite of the Japanese since ancient times as a symbol of permanence and long life owing to its strength against the cold and its eternally green branches. In the same manner, this pinestraw hue, or jade green, is prized for its connotation of vitality.

鶸色

Light Lime Green

ひわいろ

鮮やかな黄緑色。色名はスズメ目アトリ科の小鳥、ヒワのすがすがしい黄緑色の羽の色にちなむ。藍で下染して黄蘗（きはだ）で重ね染めした染色で、室町時代から使われている色名。江戸時代にはもう少し青みが強い鶸萌葱（ひわもえぎ）や、渋い茶色がかった鶸茶（ひわちゃ）などの色も生まれた。

Hiwa-iro: a vivid yellow-green. The Japanese name is taken from the small sparrow, *hiwa*, which boasts snappy, light green feathers. To reach the proper shade, fabric is bottomed with indigo, and then dyed repeatedly with the colorant from *kihada* bark. This light lime green has been called *hiwa iro* since the Muromachi period, yet the Edo period saw the birth of newer shades, such as *hiwa-maegi*, with a strong tint of blue, and *hiwa-cha*, influenced by the cool brown of roasted tea leaves.

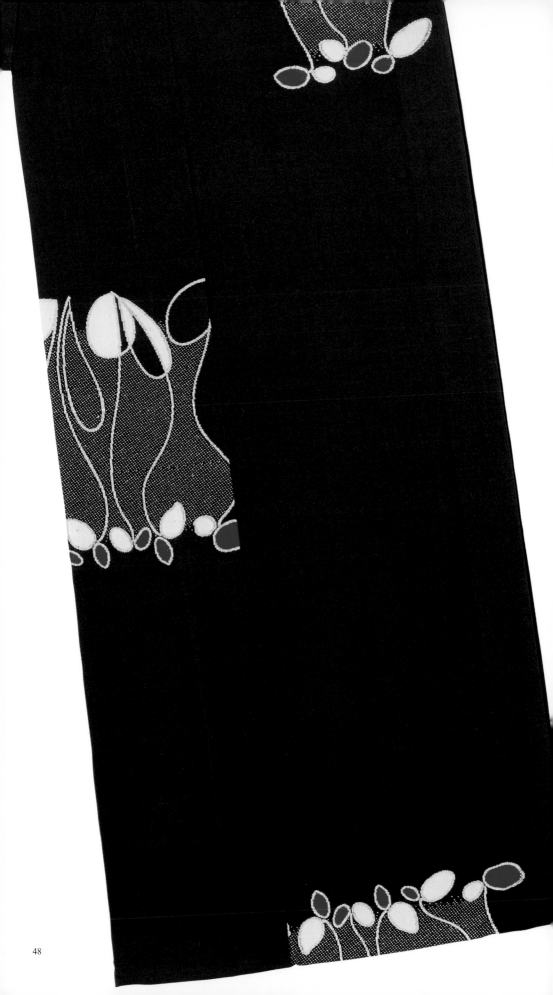

錆御納戸

Blue Conifer

さびおなんど

江戸時代の代表的な藍染の色である御納戸色のヴァリエーションのひとつで、灰色がかった青緑。「錆」は古びた、寂びた、破調の感じを表す語で、江戸中期以降、このような錆びの色の使用が、武家から民衆の間にまで浸透していき、「粋」を好む江戸人の"しぶい"という独特な色彩感覚につながった。

Sabi Onando: a blue-green tinted with gray. This *onando* variation is representative of the indigo dyes of the Edo Period. *Sabi*, literally rust, brings to mind varying images from venerable to decayed and worn down. From the middle of the period, the use of duller colors such as this trickled down from the samurai ranks to the common folk, greatly pleasing the unique sense of "subdued" colors fancied by chic Edoites.

柳鼠

Eggshell Green

やなぎねずみ

薄い緑がかったねずみ色で、「柳
の緑を含んだ鼠」の意味。江戸
時代末期から明治時代にかけて、
"鼠"を基調にした染色が見られ、
『染物早指南』(嘉永6年)に記
された46色の中で「〜鼠」とい
う色名がついているのは15種。
この破調とも言われる一般的に
クールでやわらかい色系統が「〜
鼠」と呼ばれた。

Yanagi-nezumi: a gray with a light
green haze, hinting at the image of
"gray infused with the green of a
willow." The color gray is indicated
by the suffix *nezumi* which literally
translates to "mouse." Grays were
so popular from the end of the Edo
period and into the Meiji era that
within the 46 colors described in
The Manual of Dyeing (1853), 15
of them include "-mouse" (gray)
as a suffix, which is how, with a
little stretch of the imagination,
color schemes considered cool,
yet delicate came to be called the
"mouse colors."

木賊

Spruce Green

とくさ

くすんだ青みがかった緑。多年
生常緑シダ類のトクサの茎の色
に似たことから名付けられた。こ
の色は藍の上に刈安を重ねて染
め、落ち着いた渋い緑は武家の
衣装や中年層に人気があった。
木賊色は平安時代には見られず
鎌倉時代以降に「とくさの狩衣
に青袴きたるが」(『宇治拾遺物
語』)や「木賊色の水干」(『義経
記』)などで登場する。

Tokusa: a green with a hint of
dull blue. This color got its name
from its similarity to the stem
of the scouring rush, a perennial
indeciduous fern. Spruce green,
achieved by dyeing fabric with
indigo first, then silver grass
(cayas), was particularly popular for
attire worn by samurai families and
the middle-aged populace due to its
cool and subdued ambiance. This
blackish-green hue was not evident
during the Heian period, but does
appear in literature from the end of
the Kamakura period, such as in this
quote from *A Collection of Tales
from Uji*, "...wearing a spruce-green
hunting coat and hakama" or from
Tales of Yoshitsune, "...a blackish-
green casual kimono jacket."

凛々しく成長した竹の幹のような青みの冴えた明るく濃い緑。江戸中期の文献にこの色の名前が見られるが、本格的に使われたのは明治に入ってからで、欧州から「若竹色」という染料が輸入されてからと言われる。古来から自生し、食用、楽器、建築物に使われる「竹」は生活に身近な植物だったためか「若竹色」「煤竹（すすたけ）色」「老竹色」など多彩な色名を生み出した。

Aotake-iro: a bright, deep green with a bluish hint like that of the bamboo (*take*) trunk growing graciously in the wild. Although bamboo green was mentioned a bit in literature from the middle of the Edo period, it probably wasn't until the Meiji period, when the raw umber dye arrived from Europe, that this shade found its true following. Indigenous throughout East Asia, the bamboo plant has been put to use since ancient times for daily items such as food, musical instruments, and building materials, becoming the root of a wide range of color names, including raw umber (young bamboo), brunt umber (sooty bamboo) and dark umber (old bamboo).

青竹色

Jewel Green

あおたけいろ

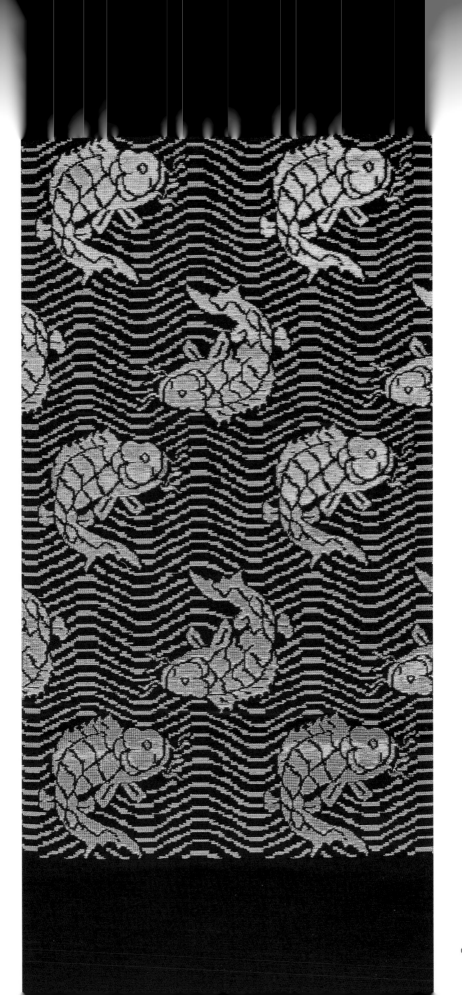

桃

Pink

ピンクと呼ばれる春の色。桃色
に染めるときに使用される紅花
はとても高価な染料であったた
めに、少量の染料で染めた桃色
のものが多い。そのため色あせ
しやすく、いつしか、男性の恋
心とかけて、「うつろいの色」と
して呼ばれるようになった。ただ、
その優しい、柔らかい、甘い色
合いは、女心そのものを象徴す
る色と言える。

Pink: the quintessential color of
spring. As the price of thistle
saffron, the base material used
for pink dyes, was so extravagant,
just a tidbit was used, resulting in
many peach and light pink colors.
The lighter shade of pink is easier
to match with other colors, and, at
some point, became known as "the
color of change," referring to a man
who has fallen in love! Yet still,
the tender, soft, sweet coloring of
pink is often used to describe a
woman's heart.

珊瑚色

Coral Pink

さんごいろ

アカサンゴの骨軸のような明るい赤色。仏教の経文の中で「七宝」のひとつとして記されている珊瑚は、海底に群をなして生活する寿命400年とも言われるサンゴ虫の死骸が、長い年月をかけて堆積したもの。江戸時代にはかんざしなどの宝飾品として人気があった。この珊瑚を粉砕したものは、中国伝来の絵の具として日本画などに用いられている。

Sango-iro: a bright red tint imitating the shade of red coral. Buddhist literature describes coral as one of the "Seven Treasures." Coral is said to have a life span of 400 years, all spent at the bottom of the ocean in large clusters. The fact is, this beautiful gem starts as a heap of coral insect skeletons, and grows over the years. Coral quickly became a treasured material for decorative hair combs and other accessories in the Edo period. Crushed coral was used in China as paint, and gradually made its way into the world of Japanese art as well.

69

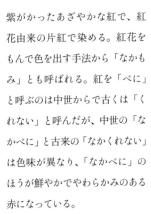

紫がかったあざやかな紅で、紅
花由来の片紅で染める。紅花を
もんで色を出す手法から「なかも
み」とも呼ばれる。紅を「べに」
と呼ぶのは中世からで古くは「く
れない」と呼んだが、中世の「な
かべに」と古来の「なかくれない」
は色味が異なり、「なかべに」の
ほうが鮮やかでやわらかみのある
赤になっている。

Nakabeni: a vivid crimson tinted
with purple, dyed in *katabeni* or a
reduced amount of safflower dye.
In Japanese, this hue is also called
nakamomi, referring to the process
of massaging the safflower to
bring out this unique shade. *Beni*
has been used to describe crimson
hues since the Middle Ages, yet
the name *kurenai* was appointed
in ancient times. Interestingly,
the shades differ within the two
time periods when the Japanese
prefix for "medium" (*naka*) is added.
Naka-beni in the Middle Ages is a
much more vibrant yet delicate red
than *naka-kurenai* of ancient times.

中紅

Cherry Pink

なかべに

鴇色

Cupid Pink

ときいろ

あかるい紫がかった赤色。トキは
現在天然記念物に指定されてい
るが、江戸時代までは全国に生
息して親しまれた鳥。体色は白
だが、飛翔した時に尾羽、風切羽、
羽の内側などが淡紅色をおびて
いる所から、紅鶴、桃花鳥とも書
かれる。別名「鴇羽色（ときはい
ろ）」で、江戸時代以降に名づけ
られた色。

Toki-iro: a reddish color tinted
with bright purple. The *toki*, or
crested ibis, is now a protected
species, but until the Edo period,
the ibis was a familiar bird found
in all parts of Japan. Although its
body is white, when in flight, its
tail feathers, flight feathers and the
inner surface of its wings display a
damask rose hue, thus the crested
ibis is also described as a red crane
and peach-blossom ibis. This cupid
pink shade was labeled *tokiwa-iro*
sometime after the Edo period.

霧島躑躅（きりしまつつじ）をイメージした紫味のある鮮やかな赤。ツツジは北半球の温暖な地方に多く分布する、春から夏にかけて咲く花。古くから庭園で栽培されるなど親しまれてきた。また、ツツジの小枝は茶色の原料として用いられており江戸時代末期には、丹波布と呼ばれる木綿と絹で織り込んだ縞布の糸はこのツツジの小枝で染められた。

Tsutsuji-iro: a brilliant purplish-red named after the Kirishima Azalea. Flourishing throughout the clement areas of the northern hemisphere, the azalea blooms from spring to summer, making it a long-standing favorite in many gardens. In addition, the azalea branches were found to be a valuable source for brown dye. From the end of the Edo period, the threads of the striped cloth known as *Tanba-fu*, a combined weave of cotton and silk, were dyed with the brown colorant created from azalea branches.

躑躅色

Azalea Pink

つつじいろ

桜
色

Very Pale Orchid Pink

さくらいろ

山桜の花を思わせる紫の薄い紅
色で、紅染めの中で最も淡い色。
「石竹」「桃」「撫子」など紅の濃
淡色と組み合わせて、能装束や
武将の小袖などにも多く使われ
た。京都に都が移された後に花
といえば桜を指すほど（それまで
は梅）桜は日本人にとって身近な
花となった。多くの歌や物語に詠
まれてきた。

Sakura-iro: the faintest of all the
crimson tints, coming from a light
crimson mixed with purple in the
image of the blossoms of the wild
cherry tree. By mixing bright red
shades such as "Chinese pink,"
"peach" and "pink," the perfect
hues for Noh costumes as well
as high-level military kimono
were achieved. Although the plum
blossom was traditionally the most
adored flower in Japan, after the
capital was moved to Kyoto, the
cherry blossom took preference,
evident not only in textiles and the
arts, but also as topics for many
songs and stories.

牡丹色

Tree Peony Pink

ぼたんいろ

紫がかった鮮やかな紅色。牡丹
は春から夏にかけて大輪の花を
咲かせる落葉低木。日本では奈
良時代の終わりころに観賞用とし
て日本庭園などに植えられた。花
色は紅、紅紫、桃色、白などが
あるが、その中の紅紫色系の花
を総称した色を牡丹色と称する。
染色として人気があったのは明
治時代の終わりごろ。

Botan-iro: a vivid red with shades
of purple. The peony tree (*botan*)
blooms in spring and summer, the
deciduous leaf bush producing
large round blossoms. The peony
was introduced to Japan during the
Nara period and quickly became
a permanent ornamental fixture
in traditional Japanese gardens.
Although the bush may boast
crimson, magenta or white flowers,
it is the magenta bloom that gives
this shade its poetic name. As a dye
for kimono, tree peony pink became
fashionable around the end of the
Meiji period.

桃の花に似たやわらかい紅色。女性らしい色合いは江戸時代には桃色木綿、桃色縮緬（ちりめん）、桃色羽二重など、女性の肌着や裏地に使われた。『萬染物張物相傳』（元禄6年）によると桃色は「かたべに（片紅）とうめむきの酢」で染めたとされる。鴇色よりもやや淡く、桜色のほうが黄味がかった色である。

Momo-iro: a soft crimson that resembles the peach blossom. This very feminine shade was common for fuchsia-colored cotton, crepe, and fine silk used for women's kimono undergarments and linings. According to the *General Textbook for Dyeing* (1693), fuchsia pink was achieved using reduced safflower dye and plum vinegar. This shade is slightly paler than cupid pink, more of a very pale orchid pink with a hint of yellow.

桃
色

Fuchsia Pink

ももいろ

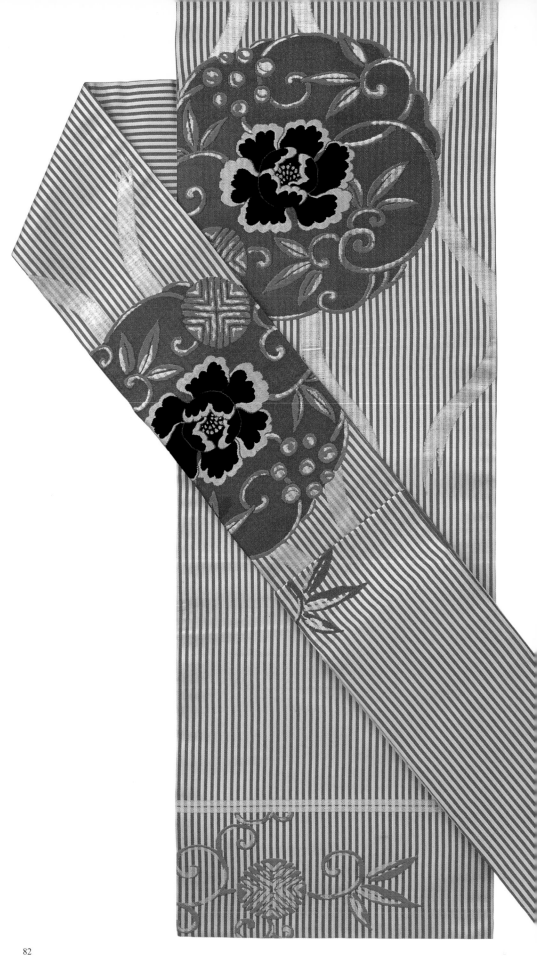

薄紅

Rose Pink

うすべに

紫をおびた淡い紅色。片紅を用
いて中紅よりもさらに淡く染め、
中紅よりも暖かみのある黄味のあ
る色となる。『燕脂染方秘傳』（文
政12年ごろ）には「下染に鬱金（う
こん）を用いて玉子色に染め、そ
れに片紅を重ねる」とある。

Usubeni: a light red tinted with
purple. Reduced safflower dye is
used to color material with a light
purple rather than a cherry pink,
creating a warm pink hue with a
yellow tint. The *Manual for Red
Dyeing* (around 1829) tells us that,
"material was bottomed with tumeric
to create the yellow hue, then layered
with reduced safflower dye."

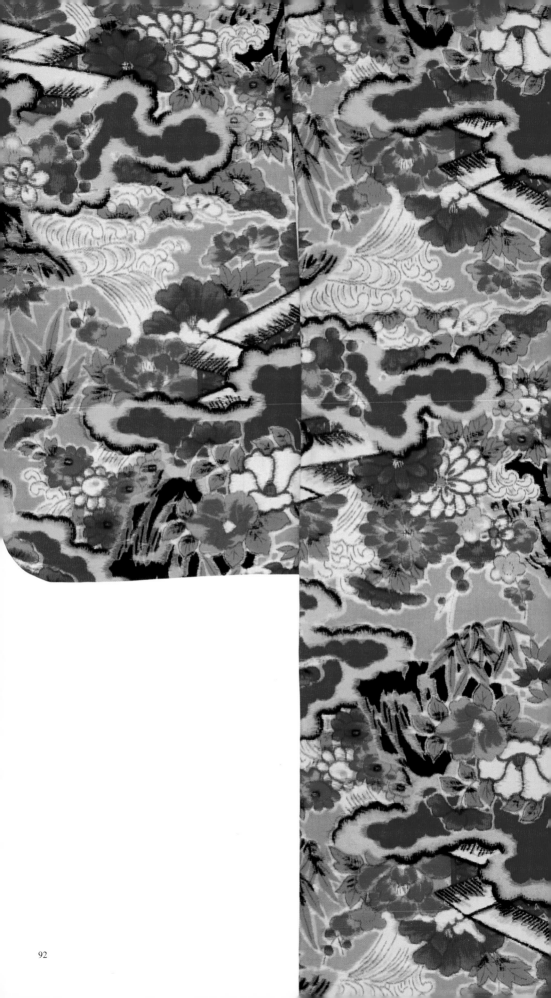

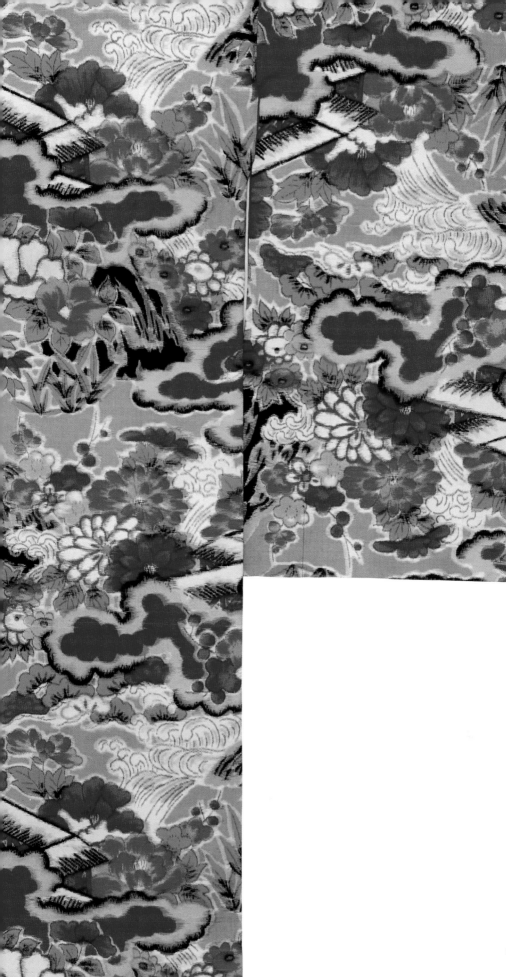

青

Blue

天空の青い空、紺碧の海、ゆる
やかに流れる大河、澄んだ湖。
人間は青色と生活をともにして
きた。だが、「青」という色を説明
するのは難しい。最も馴染みや
すい色であるがゆえに、国、時
代によって青や藍の色の認識が
異なるのである。それもあり、明
治のはじめに日本にやってきた
外国人は、日本の「青」を「ジャ
パン・ブルー」と呼んで称賛した。

The blue skies of the expansive
heavens, the cerulean ocean, a
swiftly flowing great river, a crystal
clear lake. People have always spent
their daily lives surrounded by
"blue." Yet "blue" is a very difficult
color to describe. Although it is
probably the most familiar color of
all, the recognition between blue and
indigo differ according to country
and period in history. Indeed, since
the Meiji Period visitors from
foreign countries have often admired
the blue found in Japan, enough to
nickname it, "Japan Blue."

花浅葱

Cerulean Blue

はなあさぎ

つよい緑がかった青。この花浅葱は「花色がかった浅葱色」という意味だが「花色」は鴨頭草（つきぐさ＝今の露草）の花の汁を使って染めたことに由来する。その後藍染めによる青色を「縹（はなだ）」と呼ぶようになった。文献によるとこの色の染色が行われたのは江戸末期ごろとされているが、詳細は不明。

Hana' asagi: a blue heavily tinted with green. The Japanese name indicates "a pale greenish-blue embellished with the color of flowers" telling us that the material was dyed with colorant squeezed from the dayflower (spiderwort family). Later, due to the influence of indigo dyeing, this shade came to be known as *hanada*. According to literature of the time, the dye for creating this color was developed at the end of the Edo period, but no other details are available.

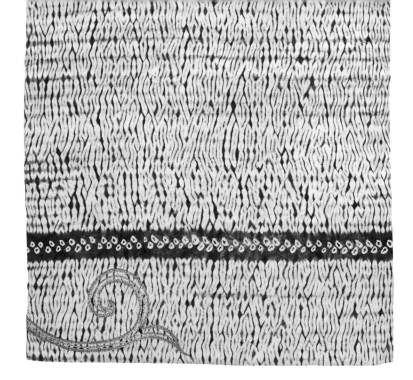

藍の単一染めの純正な青色。中
国の色名「縹」を日本では青色
の総称として用いた。あて字で
は「花田色」とも書かれるが、
これは「花色」が鴨頭草（つき
ぐさ）の花で染めたということに
由来する。『延喜縫殿式』（持統
天皇4年）によると縹は深、中、
式、浅の4級にわかれていたが
この中の「中」程度の濃さの色
だと解釈されている。

Hanada-iro: a pure blue created
with a single indigo dye. The
Japanese borrowed the Chinese
name for blue, *hanada*, to represent
all blue shades in general. Rewriting
the characters for this name
changes the meaning to "flower-
field color," also hinting that the
dye is created from the blossoms of
the dayflower (spiderwort family).
According to the *Engi Textile
Dyeing Encyclopedia* (689), blue was
divided into four categories: deep,
medium, light and pale. Sapphire
blue is interpreted as the medium
shade within the "medium" category
of blues.

縹
色

Sapphire Blue

は
な
だ
い
ろ

藍色

Marine Blue

あいいろ

タデ科の藍草の葉で染めた色の総称だが、伝統色での藍色は、藍単一染めではなく、黄蘗をかけた青緑色の色。現在のように純粋な深い青色を藍色と呼ぶようになったのは江戸時代以降になってからだ。江戸時代には手ぬぐいやのれんなどに染めて愛用されたほか、歌川広重はじめ多くの絵師が用いたことから外国では「ジャパン・ブルー」とも呼ばれていた。

Ai-iro: The word *ai* is the standard Japanese term for the well-known indigo pigment found in stems and leaves of the indigo plant (polygonacede family). However, this traditional indigo hue is not the renowned pure blue resulting from the single-stage dyeing, rather a blueish-green with a yellow tint. The pure, deep blue was not called "indigo blue" until after the Edo period. In fact, during the Edo period, due to the liberal use of deep indigo blue in *tenugui* (thin cotton hand towels) and *noren* (shop curtains), and in paintings by Japanese artists such as Hiroshige Utagawa, this shade became known as "Japan Blue" in many other countries.

新橋色

Cyan Blue

しんばしいろ

明るい緑がかった青。この「新橋」は東京の新橋のこと。当時の新橋は、実業家や政治家が訪れる新興の花柳界だった。従来の天然染料ではなく合成染料を用いたこの鮮やかな色を新橋の置屋のハイカラな芸者たちが好んだ。その置屋が今春（こんぱる）新道にあったために今春色とも言われる。対して江戸情緒を残す深川芸者が好んだ色に「深川鼠」がある。

Shinbashi-iro: a blue brightened with a hint of green. This *shinbashi* is the very Shinbashi area of Tokyo. Back in history, Shinbashi was a red-light district favored by businessmen and politicians. The elegant geisha of Shinbashi establishments cherished not the conventional natural dyes, but the synthetic dyes that created more vivid colors. A nickname for cyan blue, *konparu-iro* was a play on words mixing the meaning of spring and the name of the street where most geisha houses were located. Similarly, Edo geisha of the Fukagawa area favored the color referred to as Fukagawa Gray!

瑠璃色

Cobalt Blue

るりいろ

濃い紫を帯びた冴えた青色。仏教でも七宝とされる「瑠璃」のような青に似ていることにちなむ。瑠璃は西洋でラピスラズリと呼ばれ、西方アジアで産出され、中国を経て日本に伝わった。中国の陶器に天然の呉須に長石釉を加えることによって、青色に発色する瑠璃釉（るりゆう）がある。その技術が日本の有田焼や伊万里焼などに受け継がれてきた。

Ruri-iro: an electric blue tinted with a rich purple. The Japanese name comes from this bright blue's similarity to the color of lapis lazuli, one of Buddhism's "Seven Treasures." Called lapis lazuline in the West, this pigment was first discovered in the western part of Asia, and ultimately reached Japan through China. Chinese earthenware was decorated with natural cobalt enhanced by a feldspar glaze to create the final cobalt blue glaze. Potters of Arita and Imari inherited this special know-how and continue the process today.

浅葱色

Blue Turquoise

あさぎいろ

蓼藍で染めた薄藍色。浅葱とは
薄い葱の葉の色を意味する。古
代には刈安で染めた薄黄色の浅
黄（あさぎ）という色があったが、
平安時代にはそれが転じて「浅
葱」という色名ができたという説
もある。この色が庶民に広まった
のは江戸時代。浅葱木綿の羽織
裏を下級武士が愛用していたこ
とから吉原の遊郭では無粋なこと
を「浅葱裏」と言ってからかった。

Asagi-iro: a light indigo color
created with the indigo dye. The
Japanese name indicates the color
of the spring onion leaf. In ancient
times, silver grass (cayas) was used
to produce a pale yellow, also called
asagi. Yet during the Heian period,
the Japanese character used for the
word *asagi* was changed to fit the
blue turquoise hue. Blue turquoise
became a preference among
commoners during the Edo period.
As the lower echelon samurai
favored silky cotton in blue turquoise
for the lining of their *haori* (kimono
jackets), the derogatory term for
such visitors of the Yoshiwara red
light district was "spring onion
backs!"

紅掛空色

Salvia Blue

べにかけそらいろ

わずかな紅がかった紫みの淡い
青紫色で、別名「紅碧（べにみ
どり）」。通常「碧」は緑色を指すが、
紅碧の場合は空色を指す。空色
の上に紅色を薄く重ねた染法か
ら生まれたもので、江戸中期〜後
期に流行ったといわれるが定かで
はない。同じように二つの染料を
重ねたものに淡い紫系の色で「二
藍（ふたあい）」と鮮やかな青紫
の「紅掛花色(べにかけはないろ)」
などがある。

Benikake Sora-iro: a pale bluish
purple with just a hint of crimson,
also known as *beni-midori. Midori*
indicates green, but *beni-midori*
describes sky blue or azure. This
hue was developed by delicately
layering a crimson dye over sky
blue. It is speculated that salvia blue
became vogue around the middle of
the Edo period. Two similar colors
resulting from layered-dying are a
light purple hue called *futa'ai,* and
a brighter blue-purple known as
benikake hana-iro.

瓶覗

Horizon Blue

かめのぞき

藍染のごく淡い青色。藍で染め
たものではもっとも薄い色であ
る。「瓶」は藍の染料を入れる瓶
のことで「覗」は布などが藍瓶を
ちょっと覗く程度に浸されたとい
う説と、藍瓶に張られた水に空が
映り、それを人が覗き見るという
説のあるユニークな色名。別名「覗
色（のぞきいろ）」、または少しだ
け染まって白い布でなくなるとい
う意味で「白殺し」とも言われる。

Kame-nozoki: a very pale blue from
the indigo dye. This is probably
the lightest of all the shades dyed
with indigo. The character for *kame*
indicates the bottle that contains
the indigo dye. *Nozoki* tells us that
the cloth is just barely moistened
by the bottled indigo - the image of
catching a slight glance of the sky
reflected on the water surface in a
bottle; a unique name for a beautiful
color. In another alias, *nozoki-iro*
describes the image of a cloth that is
just slightly dyed, no longer white,
also dubbed *shiro-koroshi* or "killing
the white."

111

Brown

茶の色は、樹木の幹、土の色と
普段の暮らしの中で自然と目に
入ってくるものである。その色の
表現のもととなっているのは、お
茶の葉を焙じたときの、葉緑素
がなくなった、カフェインとタンニ
ン酸の色素だけが色として見え
るものである。庶民に飲茶の習
慣が広まったことにより、「茶色」
という表現が広まったのである。

Brown is the color of tree trunks and
soil. Brown appears to us as a bit of
nature in our daily life. The Japanese
word for brown actually means "tea;"
the color of roasted tealeaves as they
lose their chlorophyll is a soft brown.
Caffeine and tannic acid are the only
substance remaining in the leaves to
serve as pigment. As the custom of
tea drinking became popular among
the common people, the definition "the
color of tea" became popular as well.

雀茶

Brick Red

すずめちゃ

雀の頭の色のような赤黒い茶色。雀は古来より身近な鳥で、江戸時代には「吉原すずめ」のように「通」を意味する接尾語にもなっていた。これより淡く赤みがかった色を雀色ということもあるが、双方は厳密には区別されない。中国の周時代の官制を記した周礼という書物にこの色の染色の記述が雀頭色（じゃくとうしょく）としてすでに見られるが、日本では明治以降といわれる。

Suzume-cha : a brown with reddish-black tints, similar to the color of a sparrow's head. A well-loved bird from long ago, sparrow became an Edo-period suffix indicating a *connoisseur*, as in "Yoshiwara sparrow", a frequenter of the red light district. Although *suzume-cha* is also used for a slightly redder brown, the distinction is very vague. The dye is noted as early as the Zhou period (11th century to 256 BC) in China, yet not mentioned in Japan until the Meiji Period.

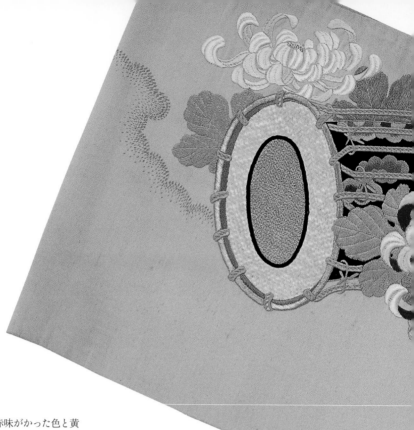

ごく薄い茶。赤味がかった色と黄
味がかった白茶も総称して白茶と
いう。丁字（ちょうじ）を使って染
める香色（こういろ）と同じ染色
法を用いる。この色が愛用された
のは元禄中期以降。当時は比較
的濃い白茶が人気だったがその
後の文化・文政の時代以降、女
性の着物などこの淡い茶色系が
愛用された。現代でも「ベージュ」
という名前で親しまれている。

Shiracha: an extremely light brown.
The name *shiracha* is used as a
general term for light brown with
either a red or yellow tint. The same
method of dyeing with cloves is used
to create both this sand beige and
a brown called *ko-iro* or "incense."
This shade became fashionable
near the end of the Genroku period
(1688-1704). At this time a stronger
light brown was the trend, but
during the Bunka-Bunsei period of
the early 1800s, women began to
favor a very pale brown. Nowadays
this shade is referred to as beige
even in Japan.

白茶

Sand Beige

しらちや

栗皮茶

Chestnut

くりかわちゃ

黒みがかった赤褐色で別名栗色、栗皮色。つややかな栗の実の皮の色に似ていることにちなむ。平安時代には『源氏物語』に「落栗とかや、昔の人のめでたしける袷（あわせ）の袴（はかま）一具」とあるが、この「落栗」はこの栗皮茶と同色と言われる。染色法は諸説があるが「栗皮染」という栗の樹皮と灰汁で茶に染める方法もある。

Kurikawacha: a shade of sienna influenced by black, also known by nut-brown and other pseudonyms having to do with the *kuri* or chestnut. The name comes from the unique sheen this shade boasts, imitating the glossy shell of the chestnut. *The Tale of Genji*, written during the Heian period, tells us "people of long ago favored the color of fallen chestnuts for their hakama pants as a part of their thick, winter kimono; essentials of full formal attire." There are many accounts on how to dye the chestnut pigment, but the most common method is called "chestnut-shell dyeing" in which a combination of chestnut bark and lye is used to achieve the proper brown hue.

緑がかった薄茶色。室町・桃山時代の茶人、千利休（1522〜91）が好んだ色とされているが、この色名が文献に現れたのが千利休死後の江戸中期ごろ。そういった時代背景から「当時の呉服屋が千利休の名を借りて流行色を作った」との説もある。この時代で緑を帯びた色には利休色、利休白茶、利休鼠など「利休」の名を冠した色も多く生まれている。

Rikyūcha: a light brown with a hint of green. This color is claimed to be the favorite of the eminent Muromachi-Momoyama period tea master Sen'norikyū (1522-91). Interestingly, *rikyūcha* as the name of a color (*rikyū* indicating the famed tea master and cha meaning tea) didn't appear in literature until after Sen'norikyū's death, around the middle of the Edo period. The theory is that kimono merchants borrowed Sen'norikyū's name, postmortem, to create a new trend from an old shade. Indeed, most shades tinted with green during this period were dubbed with the prefix *rikyū*, and many new hues were consequently fashioned, such as *rikyū-shiracha* (greenish light brown) and *rikyū-nezumi* (greenish gray).

利休茶

Dusty Olive

りきゅうちゃ

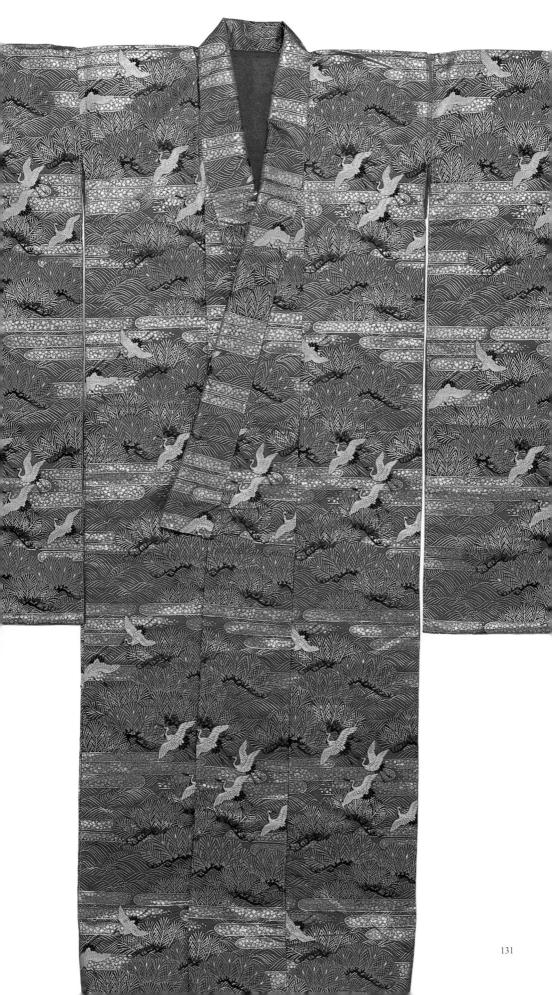

弁柄色

Copper Rust

べんがらいろ

暗い赤みを帯びた茶色。ベンガラ
は酸化第二鉄（土中の鉄が酸化し
たもの）を主成分とする顔料で、
塗料や染料として多く使われてい
る。朱（天然の硫化水銀鉱物）と
縄文時代から共に土を由来とする
染料として多く使われている。ベ
ンガラの名前はインドのベンガル
地方で良質のものが採れたことに
ちなみ、紅柄、紅殻（べにがら）
と書かれることもある。

Bengara-iro: a brown tinged with
dark red. Red-ochre, bengara, is
a pigment containing mainly ferric
oxide, an iron that is naturally
oxidized in the earth. Red-ochre
is used liberally as both a dye for
materials and a food coloring. Both
red-ochre and vermilion (natural
mercury sulfide) are the two
fundamental dyes stemming from the
earth that have been used since the
Jomon period. The name bengara,
also written as benigara, most likely
originates from the name of the
Bengal area in India, a well-known
source for high-quality red-ochre
dye.

江戸前期に流行した赤みのある茶。江戸を冠して新趣向の色であることを強調し、「当世茶」とも呼ばれた。遊廓の風俗をまとめた延宝7（1679）年の色道大鑑には、遊廓へ通う客の「帯は黒きを最上とす。茶色またよろし。茶の中にも、江戸茶、黄唐茶を制す」とある。楊梅の皮で下染めをし、蘇芳や茜で赤みを加える。

Edo Cha: a reddish-brown hue popular in the early Edo Period, nicknamed "Modern Brown" to emphasize its symbol as the color of the new Edo style. According to the Shikido Okagami, a collection of brothel etiquette (1679), the color of obi worn by clients indicated status: "Black obi is the highest rank. Brown obi is equally respected. Of the browns, Edo-cha is far superior to Kigara-cha." Achieved by dying with wild plum skin, then adding raspberry and madder.

江戸茶

Garnet Brown

えどちや

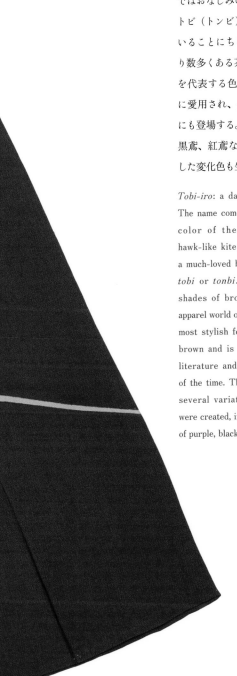

赤味の強い暗めの茶褐色。日本ではおなじみのワシタカ科の鳥、トビ（トンビ）の羽の色に似ていることにちなむ。江戸初期より数多くある茶の中でも「茶色」を代表する色として男性を中心に愛用され、多くの文学や逸話にも登場する。天明期には紫鳶、黒鳶、紅鳶などこの色を基調とした変化色も生まれた。

Tobi-iro: a dark, reddish brown. The name comes from the reddish color of the feathers of the hawk-like kite (accipitrid family), a much-loved bird in Japan, called *tobi* or *tonbi*. Among the many shades of brown favored in the apparel world of the Edo period, the most stylish for men was coconut brown and is often mentioned in literature and familiar anecdotes of the time. Throughout the 1780s, several variations of this shade were created, influenced with tinges of purple, black and red.

鳶色

Coconut Brown

とびいろ

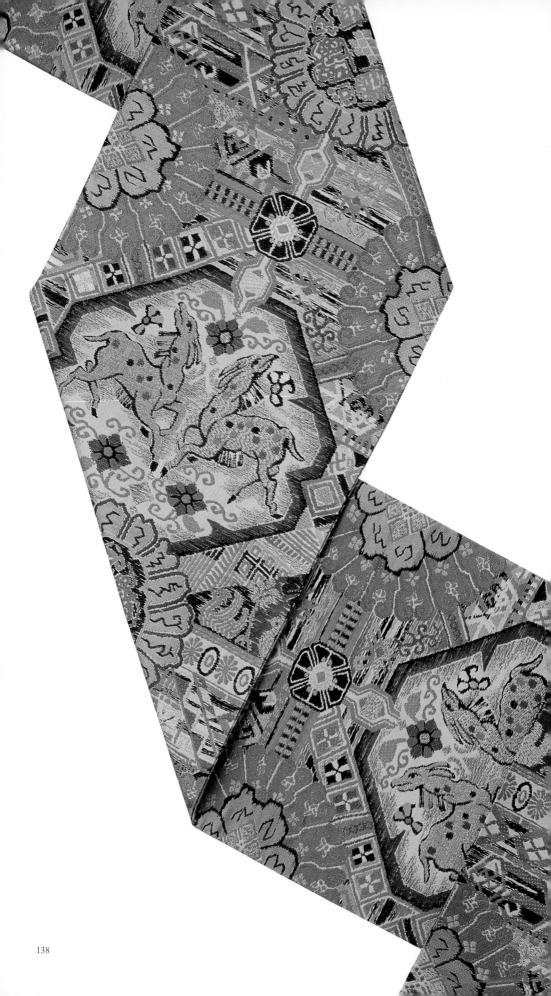

焦茶

Van Dyke Brown

こげちゃ

黒味がかった濃い茶色。ものが
焼けこげたような茶色だが、元
禄までは「焦茶」という色名の
文献が見られない。その名前が
登場するようになったのは、享
保12年の『當流模様雛形天の橋
立（とうりゅうもようひながたあ
まのはしだて）』以降のこと。ほ
うじ茶を思わせる香ばしさが漂
うような濃茶色は、現在でもな
じみ深い色でもある。

Kogecha: a dark blackish brown.
Kogecha literally means, "burnt
tea leaves." This pigmentation
was never mentioned in literature
until the Genroku period and
didn't appear in full force until 1727,
after the *Toryu Moyo Hinagata
Amanohashidate Color Book* was
published. *Kogecha* is still a favorite
dark brown hue as it reminds us of
the rich aromas of roasted green tea.

148

紫

Purple

日本の自然の中で紫の美しさを
見るのは杜若や花菖蒲が咲き競
う五月。千変万化、様々に色を
変化していく光景は、人を惑わ
せるような不思議な世界である。
紫は色の三原色からみれば間色
であるのに、古代から世界各地
で高貴な色とされているのは、
紫の持つ妖艶さ、神秘性とも言
える人を吸いつけるような魅力
のためなのかもしれない。

Purple is most often spotted in
Japan in the month of May, when
the rabbit-ear iris and Japanese iris
rival each other with their gorgeous
blossoms. A spectacle that changes
colors like a kaleidoscope, purple
has been a color of royalty from
ancient times throughout the world.
Perhaps this royal aura of purple is
due to its fascinating and mystical
charm, luring people into its power.

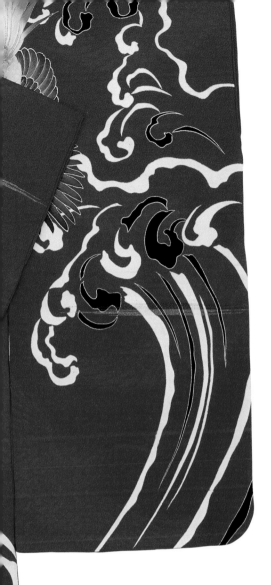

牡丹

Fuchsia Purple

ぼたん

紫がかったあざやかな赤色。色名は牡丹の花びらの色に似ていることにちなむ。大振りの花を咲かせる艶やかな牡丹の花は、中国では6世紀ころから観賞用として珍重され、「富貴な花」と呼ばれた。日本に入ってきたのは奈良時代の終わりごろと遅く、牡丹色が日本の文献に登場するのは平安時代末の頃。

Botan: a vivid red tinted with purple, named after its similarity to the color of peony petals. The lustrous bloom of the peony sprouting from the end of lanky branches came to be prized as an ornamental flower in China during the 6th century, and was quickly nicknamed "the wealthy flower." The peony arrived in Japan rather late, around the end of the Nara period, and the name *botan* didn't actually appear in literature until the end of the Heian period.

153

深紫

Deep Royal Purple

こきむらさき

紫紺（しこん）、灰汁、酢を用い
て染めた、黒みがかった深い紫
色。「衣服令」の定めでは、この
深紫は一位の衣の色で、他のも
のへの着用が許されない禁色（き
んじき）とされた。平安時代に
は清少納言が「すべて、なにも
なにも、紫なるものは、めでたく
こそあれ。花も、糸も、神も」と
詠んだことからも、その紫を尊
ぶ心や風潮は時代を超えて伝え
られている。

Koki-murasaki: a deep purple tinged
with black, the hue achieved by
blending a purple dye with lye and
vinegar. According to the dress
code of the time, this deep purple
was limited to kimono for the
highest-ranking persons only and
prohibited from use by the lower
echelons. In the Heian period, Sei
Shonagon, author of *The Pillow
Book*, wrote that "in any and all
cases, purple is the expression of
happiness and good things. Even the
flowers, the threads, and the gods."
A climate of true respect toward
purple has been brought down the
ages.

155

紫紺

Blackish Purple

しこん

濃い紺色を帯びた暗めの紫。色
名の紫紺はムラサキソウ（紫草）
の根で染めた色だったことから
紫根と書かれた。これが紫紺と
なったのは明治以降のこと。江
戸時代以前には染色本などの文
献にこの色名ではでてこない。
天皇即位の礼の幡（ばん）でも
用いられたが、現代ではその荘
厳な色調を尊んで、優勝旗の色
として広く親しまれている。

Shikon: a dark purple influenced
with a dense navy. The name *shikon*
originates from the dyeing method
using the root of the purple grass;
shi means purple and *kon* means
root. The name shikon was used
only after the Meiji period, and
was never mentioned in dyeing-
related literature prior to the Edo
period. This blackish-purple was
used for the congratulatory flags
flown for imperial coronations and
continues to be highly revered for
its stateliness, often the selected
coloring for championship flags.

わずかに赤または紫がかった濃い藍色で、藍の単一染の中で最も濃い色。中国古来の色名だった紺が日本に渡ったのは孝徳天皇大化3年の七色十三階冠位の制「紺＝ふかきはなだ」から。木綿が普及するようになった桃山から江戸時代にかけて藍染が盛んになり、紺染めを専門とした「紺屋（こうや）」なども登場するなど、大衆的な色として人々に愛された。

Kon: a deep indigo color with just a bit of red or purple tint, certainly the deepest of the single-dye indigo shades. Although purple-navy existed in ancient China, it didn't arrive in Japan until during the rule of Emperor Kotoku. The *Thirteen Rank Color Designation System* (published in 647) designated each rank one of seven colors, including purple-navy (referred to as *fukaki-hanada*). Cotton was the favored fabric from the Momoyama to Edo periods, particularly for indigo dyeing. The popularity of the material and color lead to the establishment of *koya*, literally "houses of navy," specializing in purple-navy dyeing.

紺

Purple Navy

こん

似紫

Plum

にせむらさき

くすんだ青みの赤紫。紫根を使っ
た本紫に似せた色という意味。
高貴な色とされ、紫が禁色だっ
た時代を経て、鎌倉時代には次
第にさまざまな色が開放されて
いった。しかし、寛永20年以降
には、庶民が高価な紫根（＝本
紫)を使うことが禁じられたため、
藍で染めた上に茜や蘇芳を重ね
て染めた似せ紫など、染法によっ
てその色を模した色が登場した。

Nise murasaki: a red-purple subdued
with blue. *Nise* means an imitation
and *murasaki* means purple, so
named because the dye was created
to imitate the dye made from the
actual root of the *murasaki* plant
(lithospermi radix). As purple was
considered a color for nobility, it
was barred from use by the common
people until finally, in the Kamakura
period (1185-1333), various shades
of purple were released to the public
for general use. However, from
1643, the common people were again
barred from using the precious
murasaki root (pure purple), and
they resorted to using indigo,
layered with madder and raspberry
red dye to create "fake" purples
such as this plum.

桔梗色

Violet

ききょういろ

桔梗の花びらを思わせる冴えた
濃い青紫。秋の七草の一つでも
ある桔梗は8月〜9月にかけて
釣り鐘型の美しい花を開く。染
料は藍で染めた後に紅花を重ね
て染めるが、同じ素材で染める
二藍（ふたあい）よりも青みを
強調するのが特徴。近松の『女
殺油地獄』（享保6年）では「桔
梗染の腰変わり縞襦の帯」との
くだりで桔梗染が登場する。

Kikyo-iro: a rich blue-violet hue
that immediately brings to mind
Chinese bellflower petals. The
Chinese bellflower is one of the
seven autumnal flowers that boast
beautiful blossoms in the shape of
temple bells between August and
September. Fabric is dyed with
indigo first, and then layered with
the safflower dye. Rather than
dyeing with the *futa ai* double-
layer indigo, this method achieves
a stronger blue. In playwright
Chikamatsu's *The Woman-Killer*,
(1721), he described, "a *kikyo-zome*
obi in a crisscross pattern," giving
us the first mention of this violet
shade in the literature of the time.

赤味がかった黒、または黒味が
かった赤。染料は紅染に檳榔子
（びんろうじ）を重ねて黒味をか
けたもので、黒紅梅（くろこうば
い）とも呼ばれる。西鶴の『萬
の文反古（よろずのふみほうぐ）』
では「御内儀の昔小袖…黒紅に
御所車の縫箔の小袖」というく
だりがあることからも、江戸前期
から高価な小袖の地色として使
われていることがわかる。

Kurobeni: a reddish-black or
blackish-red. The dye used to make
this shade is a layering of crimson
and colorant from the Betel nut
palm tree, which gives it the black
tint and the nickname *kurokoubai*,
meaning black-red plum. Found
on scrap paper of Ihara Saikaku's
writings was a note describing, "the
proprietress's traditional kimono...a
dusky purple kimono embroidered
with a gold brocaded court carriage,"
showing us that even from the early
Edo period, dusky purple was used
for the background color of fancy
kimono.

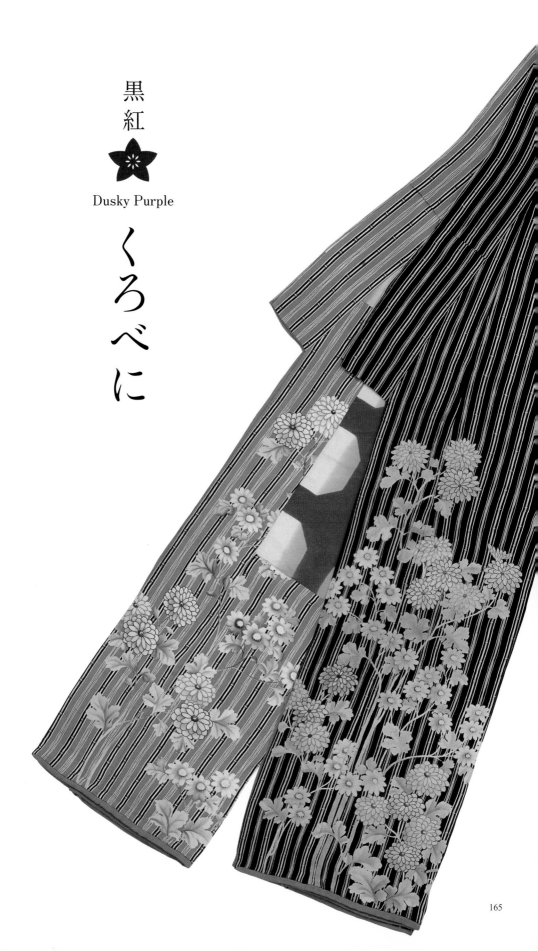

黒紅

Dusky Purple

くろべに

菖蒲色

Iris

しょうぶいろ

鮮やかな青味を帯びた紫。水辺に生育する菖蒲の花びらの色に似ていることにちなむ。あやめ（＝ハナショウブ）いろと呼ぶこともある。もとは2色を合わせた襲（かさね）の色で「表青、裏紅梅」または「表淡萌葱、裏濃紅梅」となっているが、これは葉の間にある肉穂花をつけた菖蒲草の色。現在菖蒲色と呼ばれる紫色となったのは江戸時代後期から。

Shobu-iro: a purple tinged with a brilliant blue, named after the petals of the iris, a plant always found by the water's edge. Iris, both the color and the flower, are also called *ayame* and *hanashobu* in Japanese. Originally, iris was produced as a double color with either a blue front and a crimson-plum back or a light green front and a deep crimson-plum back. However, this particular shade was created using the spadix found between the iris leaves. The iris color we know today was established during the second half of the Edo period.

黄

Yellow

黄色は明るくあたたかい光を
放って人間の眼を強く引きつけ
る色である。黄色は古くから歴
史上に登場してきて、仏教伝来
以降の経典の写経に用いられた
手漉和紙は、その多くが白紙で
はなく黄蘗で染められていた。こ
れは黄蘗に防虫効果があるため
で、あわせて黄色が墨の色の美
しさをより深める点にもある。高
貴な色として尊ばれてきた。

Yellow gives off a bright, warm
light that the human eye draws in
hungrily, and has been mentioned
throughout the analogs of history.
Handmade rice paper used for
copying the sutras, ancient Buddhist
scriptures, was most often not a
plain white, but dyed yellow. Dying
paper yellow not only served as an
insect repellant, but also made the
color of the India ink ever so richer.
The color of yellow has always been
regarded as a noble color.

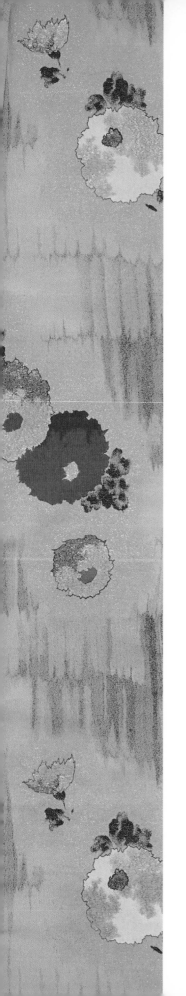

藤黄

Sunflower

とうおう

曖昧の冴えた黄色で、黄色の顔
料、藤黄の色にちなむ。藤黄は
ビルマやタイなどに生育する、オ
トギリソウ科の海藤（かいとう）
の樹液を集めて固めたもので毒
性がある。古くはフランドル（ベ
ルギー）の画家たちが好んで使用
した顔料で、日本でも江戸時代に
は友禅染で欠かせない顔料とし
て、また明治期には、日本画や洋
画の絵の具として広く使われた。

Tou'ou: a rather vague yellow. The
Japanese name comes from the
yellow wisteria pigment. Yellow
wisteria is native to Myanmar
and Thailand. A member of the
guttiferae family, the yellow wisteria
becomes toxic when the sap (*kaito*)
is extracted and hardened. This
pigment was a favorite with the
Flanders artists and was considered
an indispensable colorant in the Edo
period for yuzen dyeing, eventually
becoming widely used in both
Japanese and Western style painting
in the Meiji period.

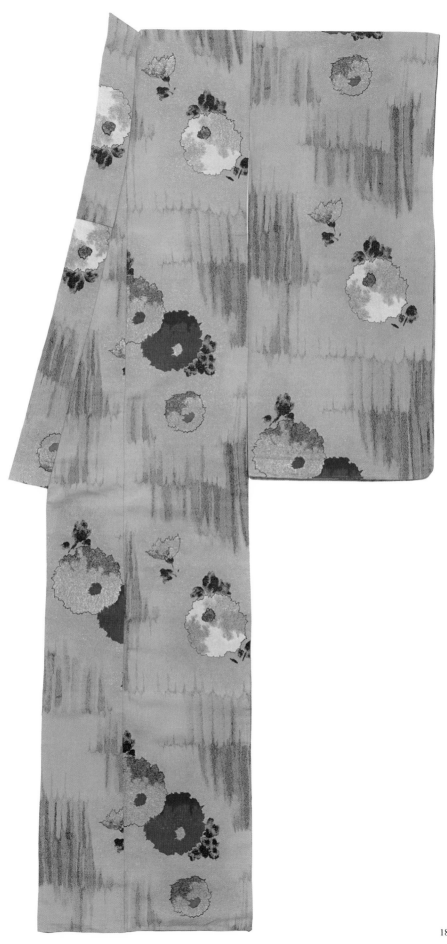

蒸栗色

Chartreuse Yellow

むしくりいろ

緑がかった淡い黄色。蒸した栗
の実のようにやわらかい色にに
ていることにちなむ。この染色が
文献に登場するのは中国の古代
書『璽雅（じが）』が最古だとさ
れているが、これによると「蒸栗」
の色が、日本で一般的に思われ
ている色と違うという説もある。
日本ではいつからこの色が登場
したかは定かではない。

Mushikuri-iro: a light yellow with a
touch of green. The Japanese name
adeptly describes this hue as the
color of a steamed chestnut. This
dye first appears in the ancient
Chinese document *Jiga* as the oldest
chartreuse, yet it is also said that
this may not be the same shade
as what is generally considered
"steamed chestnut" in Japan. It
is unclear as to when chartreuse
yellow was first used in Japan.

やや青みがかった明るい黄緑色。
染色は深山に自生するミカン科
の樹木、黄蘗の内皮を原料とし、
その煎じ汁に灰汁を加えて染め
る。古来から薬としても珍重され
ており、煎じ汁を煮詰めたものは
陀羅尼助（だらにすけ）という胃
腸薬となる。また、紙に塗ると虫
除けになることから、すでに飛鳥
時代から写経用の紙は黄蘗で染
めて使われていたという。

Kihada: a bright yellow-green lightly tinted with blue. The pigment is taken from the inner-bark of the mandarin orange tree that grows wild in the mountains. The extracted liquid is combined with lye to create a dye. Highly valued for medicinal purposes since long ago; the extract is boiled down to create a stomach remedy called daranisuke. In addition, the extract was used since the Asuka period (592-645) to dye scrolls used for copying sutras, serving as a natural insect repellent.

黄蘗

Lemon Yellow

きはだ

桑染

Maize

くわぞめ

褐色を帯びたくすんだ黄色で、
別名桑色、桑茶。養蚕の桑の樹
皮などを煎じた汁に灰汁を用い
て染める。中国伝来の伝統的な
単一染法だが、桑の木に黄の色
素が少なく何度も繰り返し染めつ
ける手間で、色としては定着しな
かったようだ。「衣服令」では黄よ
り上位の色として登場するが、そ
の後「延喜式」では色が採用され
なかったことからもうかがえる。

Kuwazome: a dull yellow tinged with
brown, also known as mulberry (*kuwa*)
or mulberry brown (*kuwacha*). The
bark of the mulberry tree, essential
to silkworm cultivation, is infused
and the extracted material mixed
with lye for dyeing. Introduced
from China, this shade is achieved
through the traditional single-dye
method, although the mulberry tree
yellow pigment is weak, requiring
several dye processes to reach the
proper shade for maize, perhaps
the reason for its lack of popularity.
According to the *Ifukurei* dress
code, maize was considered superior
to yellow, yet colors were not
employed in the *Engishiki Code of
Laws* published later on, and the
shade never made much history.

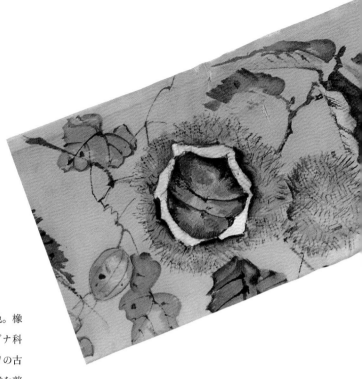

橡で染めた白茶色に近い色。橡
とは柏、楢、櫟、樫などブナ科
の木の実のことで、ドングリの古
名。しかし、古来からこの橡を煎
じて染めた白茶の衣類は、低い
身分のものの衣服や喪服として
のみ使われた。白橡の名は正倉
院古文書に多く出てくるが、それ
も「公私奴隷や女従が着用する
色」となっている。日本の身分制
度の歴史を物語る色だと言える
だろう。

Shiro tsurubami: similar to a
white-brown, dyed with the shell
of the horse chestnut. *Tsurubami*
belongs to the beech family, along
with the daimyo oak, Japanese
oak, evergreen oak, and Japanese
chestnut oak and is also an ancient
word for "acorn." In ancient times
black-brown kimono dyed with the
chestnut extract were only used by
the lower classes or for mourning
attire. The name *shiro tsurubami*
appears in ancient Shosoin archives
yet is described as "a color only
to be worn by public and private
slaves and low-ranking women."
Flax is certainly a color that clearly
illustrates the history of the class
system in Japan.

白橡

Flax

しろつるばみ

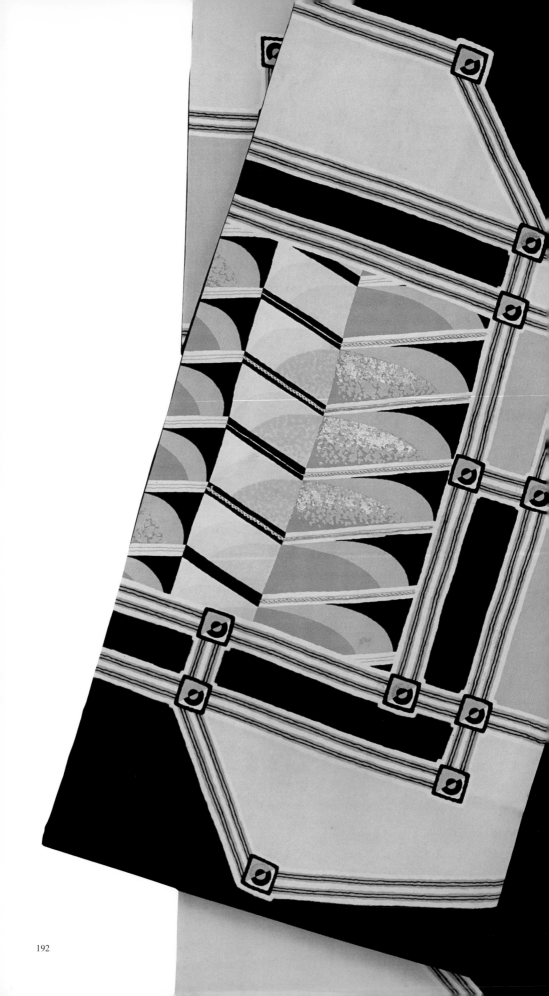

194

黒白

Black & White

「白」は自然界においては雪や霜、霧などで表わされ、どのような色にも染まるところから、清らかで、汚れのないものの象徴として使用されている。その対極にある色としてとらえられているのが「黒」。人は暗闇を恐れながらも、その中にすべての色が内包されるように感じて、墨の中にすべての、あらゆる色が含まれているとも説いた。

White symbolizes so much of the natural world-snow, frost, fog, and more. It can be dyed into any other color on the spectrum. Its pure and pristine appearance makes it customary for use on many occasions. At the other end of the spectrum is black, the color that represents the darkness that humans fear so much. Yet we also sense that black holds all the colors of the universe, just as we have been taught that India ink too, is home to all colors.

漆を塗ったようにつややかな黒い色で、真の黒のことを「漆黒」と表現することも多い。「けれども其一重瞼の中に輝く瞳子（ひとみ）は漆黒であった」（『明暗』夏目漱石）「下まぶたから漆黒な線が、口に向いてイナヅマ状にはしっていた」（『女ひと』室生犀星）など、特に近代作家が、闇、髪、瞳などの黒を表す情緒的な表現として愛用してきた色。

Shikkoku: a glossy black that looks like freshly painted lacquer. The name of this shade in Japanese, *shikkoku*, indicates that this is a true black, or "lacquer black," a favorite expression of modern writers for describing the blackness of many objects such as the dark, hair, and pupils. In *Light and Darkness*, Natsume Soseki writes, "Yet her single-edged eyelids unveiled sparkling pupils of lacquer black." In Muroi Saisei's *The Woman*, running mascara is described as "a line of lacquer black running from her lower eyelid toward her mouth like a lightening bolt."

漆黒

Lamp Black

しっこく

白・白練

Snow White

しろ・しろねり

「白」はあらゆる波長の可視光線を反射する色で、最も明るい色。ここで言う「しろ」は素色（しろいろ）、乳色など白に近い色の総称。本来「白練」は絹の黄味を消す精錬法であるが、絹を白練した色を「白」と呼ぶ。光沢のある絹の純白は古代では神聖さを象徴する色として珍重されたが、近年になって清潔で高貴な色として愛用されるようになった。

Shiro, Shiro-neri: White is the brightest color of all, reflecting the rays of all visible light. The term *shiro* used here indicates a general name for any shade close to white, such as ivory and milky white. *Shironeri*, refers to the method of refinement that rids silk of its natural yellowish tone, and the color of such refined silk is called *shiro*, or white. The pure white of lustrous silk was highly treasured as a sacred color from ancient times, yet is now valued more for its symbolism of purity and cleanliness.

墨
色

Charcoal Gray

すみいろ

茶を含んだ濃い灰黒色。古来か
ら僧侶の常服の色、または凶事
を表す色とされたが、近代に入る
と装飾としての墨色が普及した。
飛鳥時代には水面に流した墨汁
文様を写し取る「墨流染」など
雅で芸術的な染色法なども生ま
れた。「墨染」は墨を使うだけで
なく、橡（つるばみ）の樹木、檳
榔子（びんろうじ）など、時代に
よって様々な素材が使われた。

Sumi-iro: a deep ash-black tinged
with brown. Long recognized as the
color of a monk's everyday robes,
as well as the symbol of a looming
disaster, this somber color has
also grown to be valued in more
ornamental and fashionable realms.
An elegant and highly artistic
method of black ink dyeing called
bokuryu-zome was discovered in
the Asuka period which involved
capturing patterns of India ink
floating on the water's surface. Yet
ink dyeing did not only involve India
ink; a variety of materials were
used throughout the ages, such as
chestnut tree and the Betel nut palm.

白鼠

Pearl Gray

しろねずみ

しろねずとも呼ばれる銀色のようなごく明るい灰色、別名銀色（しろがねいろ）。墨の濃淡を示す「墨の五彩」焦、濃、重、淡、清の中での「清」にあたり、一番淡い色である。黒・白を基調とした「鼠」の名前がつく色は色の薄い方から白鼠、銀鼠（ぎんねず）、素鼠（すねず）、丼鼠（どぶねず）となっている。

Shiro-nezumi: a very bright gray, close to the color of silver, also known as *shirogane-iro*. Among the "Five Colors of Gray" used to describe the various shades - burnt, dark, solemn, pale, pure - pearl gray (literally "white mouse" in Japanese) fits under the faintest category of all. When the suffix *nezumi* or *nezu* or is added to a color name, it indicates that gray and white have been balanced to create a lighter shade, such as pearl gray (*shiro-nezumi*), silver gray (*gin-nezu*), ivory gray (*su-nezu*) and dark gray (*dobu-nezu*).

藍 墨 茶

Dark Slate

あいすみちゃ

藍色を帯びた墨色で、相済茶と書かれることもある。この「茶」は茶色を表すのではなく、「暗くくすんだ色合い」という意味合い。名前の由来は「(前略)このいろをあらたにそめさせ、着そろへたりしより、あゐすみ茶の名ここにはじまれり」と『手鑑模様節用』の文献に記されたことにちなむ。渋みのある色合いは、質実剛健を尊んだ享保の時代に愛用された。

Aisumi-cha: a charcoal gray enhanced with indigo. Unlike most color names, this *cha* does not indicate brown, but a blackish, dim blend. A possible origin of the name was found in a quote from the *Tekagami Moyo Setuyo*, "...the name *aisumi-cha* was determined from the habit of re-dyeing kimono fabric after several usages, adjusting to the proper shade." Dark slate was popular during the Kyohō era (1716-36) for its austere elegance and masculinity.

214

金銀

Gold & Silver

中世から近世にかけては、日本
はイタリアの旅行家マルコ・ポー
ロをして「黄金の国、ジパング」
と言わしめるほど豊かな金の生
産量を誇っていた。漆に金銀の
装飾を施した蒔絵がその頃より
盛んに行なわれるようになって、
はるかヨーロッパからやってきた
南蛮人の眼をとらえたのである。
威厳を示す豪華絢爛さの象徴と
して、時の権力者たちに用いら
れた色である。

From the Middle Ages to modern
times, Japan took such pride in
their plentiful production of gold
that Marco Polo, the great Italian
adventurer, labeled it, "Zipangu, the
country of gold!" The liberal use of
gold and silver embellishments on
Japanese lacquerware flourished
rapidly and caught the eyes of the
many foreign visitors from Europe
long ago. The luxurious splendor
gold and silver bring about has a
certain dignity, making them popular
colors among the rich and affluent
classes.

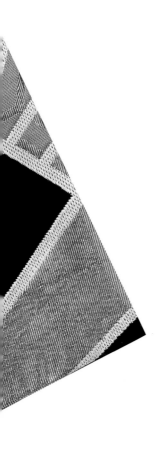

金色

Gold

きんいろ

こんじき、こがねとも称される光沢のある独特の美しい黄色。『後漢書東夷伝』によると、日本が初めて金と出会ったのは1世紀に光武帝が倭国に金印を送った時とされている。また、日本で金が発掘されたのは8世紀ごろ。それ以降金箔、摺箔（すりはく）、金襴など安土桃山時代には権力を示す装飾品として必要不可欠な色であった。

Kin-iro: a rare and beautiful, lustrous yellow, also known as *konjiki* and *kogane*. According to the *Historical Records of the Eastern Han Dynasty*, Chinese Emperor Guang Wu Di introduced gold to Japan in the first century with a gift of gold seal. Gold was actually discovered and excavated in Japan in the 8th century. By the Azuchi-Momoyama period (1568-1603), valuables such as gold leaf, *surihaku* (printed gold foil), and gold brocade became popular ornaments, and eventually, the color of gold became an essential displays of wealth and power in various adornments.

銀色

Silver

ぎんいろ

美しい金属光沢を持った青白色で、白金（しろがね）とも言われる。金は太陽、銀は月と称されるように古来から愛されてきた金属。日本では朝鮮半島より輸入され、7世紀には対馬から銀が産出されるようになった。『万葉集』の有名な歌に「銀（しろかね）も金（くがね）も玉も何せむに勝れる宝子に及（し）かめやも」（山上憶良）と詠まれている。

Gin-iro: a bluish-white hue with a beautiful metallic luster, also known as *shirogane*, or platinum. Silver has been favored just as much as gold since ancient times, when gold was lovingly considered the sun and silver, the moon. Silver was first imported from Korea, but excavation began in Tsushima in the seventh century. As recited in a famous poem from *Manyōshu*, "even more valuable than silver and gold and gems, our children are our treasures..." (Yamanoue no Okura).

223

着 物 の 案 内

Kimono Guide

P5

時代　昭和初期
図柄　百花繚乱
　　　唐織丸帯

P13

時代　大正期
生地　縮緬
図柄　松ヶ枝
技法　型友禅
　　　小振袖

P14-15

時代　昭和後期
生地　鬼縮緬
図柄　花筏
技法　友禅
　　　振袖

P16-17

時代　江戸後期
生地　緋縮緬
図柄　春の七草
技法　刺繍
　　　小袖

P18-19

時代　昭和初期
生地　縮緬
図柄　松竹梅鶴亀有職
技法　総刺繍
　　　打掛け

P20

時代　昭和中期
図柄　椿に尾長鳥
　　　綾織袋帯

P22-23

時代　明治期
生地　縮緬と紬地
図柄　菊
技法　型友禅
　　　中着

P24-25

時代　昭和中期
図柄　有職唐草
　　　更紗名古屋帯

P26-27

時代　昭和初期
生地　紋綸子
図柄　花筏
　　　長襦袢

P28-29

時代　明治期
生地　平絹に縮緬
図柄　観世水に楓
技法　型染め
　　　中着

P30

時代　大正期
図柄　牡丹に尾長鳥
　　　唐織丸帯

P31

時代　大正期
生地　縮緬
図柄　松竹梅吉祥高砂
技法　総刺繍
　　　打掛け

P32-33

時代　昭和初期
生地　繻子
技法　友禅に刺繍
　　　打掛け

P33

時代　大正期
生地　紋縮緬
図柄　七宝に四季折枝
技法　絞りに総刺繍
　　　襦袢

P34

時代　昭和中期
図柄　市松取り
　　　青海波に松
　　　唐織丸帯

P35

時代　昭和中期
図柄　椿唐草
　　　唐織袋帯

P36

時代　昭和中期
生地　紋綸子
図柄　光琳梅
技法　型友禅
　　　長襦袢

P37

時代　大正期
生地　紋綸子
図柄　壷垂に糸菊
技法　型友禅に刺繍
　　　訪問着

P40-41

時代　昭和初期
生地　一越縮緬
図柄　松林に短歌
技法　友禅
　　　訪問着

P43

時代　昭和初期
生地　繻子
図柄　黒縞に紅葉
技法　型とま描
　　　訪問着

P44-45

時代　昭和初期
生地　縮緬
図柄　猫柳
技法　友禅
　　　訪問着

P46-47

時代　昭和初期
生地　紋綸子
図柄　御簾に吹き寄せ
技法　友禅
訪問着

P48-49

時代　昭和中期
生地　お召し
図柄　ヌーボー草花
技法　織り

P51

時代　昭和中期
生地　お召し
図柄　市松匹田に薔薇
技法　織り

P52-53

時代　昭和初期
生地　一越縮緬
図柄　夫婦孔雀
技法　友禅
振袖

P54-55

時代　昭和初期
図柄　紅葉に波紋
紗名古屋帯

P56

時代　昭和初期
生地　紋綸子
図柄　御所解に楽器
技法　友禅に刺繍
打掛け

P57

時代　昭和初期
生地　紋紗
図柄　菖蒲原に鷺
技法　地描友禅
訪問着

P58-59

時代　昭和中期
生地　一越縮緬
図柄　唐獅子牡丹に笹
技法　友禅
色留袖

P58-59

時代　昭和中期
図柄　鸚鵡丸紋に瑞雲
唐織丸帯

P60

時代　昭和初期
図柄　匹田絞りに
　　　花盛船
刺繍名古屋帯
（元は丸帯）

P61

時代　昭和中期
図柄　荒磯
唐織袋帯

P62

時代　大正期
図柄　源氏香に百花
唐織丸帯

P62-63

時代　大正期
生地　紋綸子
技法　友禅
重ね訪問着

P64

時代　昭和初期
図柄　揚羽蝶
唐織丸帯

P64-65

時代　昭和中期
図柄　有職花
唐織袋帯

P65

時代　昭和中期
図柄　露芝
絽丸帯

P68-69

時代　昭和初期
生地　紋綸子
図柄　花筏
技法　友禅
訪問着

P70-71

時代　昭和初期
生地　紋綸子
図柄　有職唐草に
　　　牡丹と桐
技法　型友禅
付け下げ

P72

時代　明治期
生地　縮緬
図柄　昔話
技法　型友禅
中着

P74-75

時代　昭和中期
技法　友禅
訪問着

P76

時代　昭和初期
図柄　松に鳳凰と鼓
綴丸帯

P79

時代　昭和初期
生地　一越縮緬
図柄　渓谷山景
技法　地描
訪問着

P81

時代　大正期
図柄　波に飛鶴
唐織丸帯

P82

時代　昭和初期
図柄　立涌に有職花
繻子地名古屋帯

P84

時代　昭和初期
生地　銘仙
図柄　唐草宝相華
技法　織り

P84

時代　昭和中期
図柄　壺に牡丹
唐織袋帯

P85

時代　大正期
図柄　桐
唐織丸帯

P85

時代　昭和初期
図柄　文庫に草花
綴刺繍丸帯

P86

時代　昭和後期
生地　銀糸入り
技法　友禅に刺繍
振袖

P87

時代　昭和初期
生地　縮緬
図柄　萩影に百合
技法　友禅
振袖

P88

時代　明治初期
生地　縮緬
図柄　菊
技法　型友禅
中着

P89

時代　昭和初期
生地　綸子
図柄　宝船に竜宮
技法　友禅に刺繍
打掛け

P90-91

時代　昭和初期
図柄　遠州七宝
唐織丸帯

P90-91

時代　昭和初期
図柄　流水に花
染め昼夜帯

P92-93

時代　昭和初期
生地　銘仙
図柄　波雲取りに百花
技法　織り

P96-97

時代　昭和中期
生地　縮緬
図柄　秋の草木
技法　友禅
訪問着

P98-99

時代　昭和初期
生地　紋綸子
図柄　葵唐草
技法　板絞りに刺繍
名古屋帯

P100-101

時代　明治初期
生地　縮緬
図柄　御所解
技法　友禅に刺繍
振袖

P102-103

時代　昭和中期
生地　一越縮緬
図柄　薔薇
技法　友禅
訪問着

P104-105

時代　昭和中期
図柄　モダン花
紗名古屋帯

P106-107

時代　明治
生地　縮緬
図柄　有職雪輪に桜
中着

P109

時代　昭和後期
図柄　瑞雲
唐織名古屋帯

P110-111

時代　江戸末期
生地　縮緬
技法　友禅に刺繍
図柄　地紙に草花
子供着物

P112-113

時代　江戸末期
生地　唐織
図柄　有職丸紋に菊
打掛け

P112-113

時代　江戸末期
生地　縮緬
技法　友禅に刺繍
打掛け

P114-115

時代　昭和後期
図柄　卍渦巻き
唐織名古屋帯

P115

時代　昭和中期
図柄　梅の木に尾長鳥
唐織袋帯

P116

時代　明治初期
生地　縮緬
図柄　御所解に
　　　吉祥鶴亀
技法　友禅に刺繍
打掛け

P117

時代　江戸後期
生地　綸子
図柄　風景
技法　総刺繍
小袖

P118

時代　昭和初期
生地　紋綸子
図柄　青地暈し
　　　梅枝に源氏香
技法　型友禅
小紋

P118-119

時代　江戸期
生地　絽
図柄　松皮菱に草花
技法　友禅に刺繍
振袖

P119

時代　大正期
図柄　松皮菱に笹と桐
唐織丸帯

P120-121

時代　大正期
生地　一越縮緬
図柄　御所解
技法　友禅に刺繍
小振袖

P121

時代　大正期
図柄　竹に雀
縮緬昼夜帯

P124

時代　昭和初期
生地　天蚕糸入り
　　　一越縮緬
図柄　東屋に鳥
技法　友禅
訪問着

P126-127

時代　大正期
図柄　千代の冠と
　　　雅楽器
綴丸帯に刺繍

P128-129

時代　大正期
図柄　市松に独楽
刺繍子供帯

P131

時代　江戸期
生地　織
図柄　松に飛鶴
打掛け

P132

時代　昭和後期
図柄　狩猟紋
綾織袋帯

P134-135

時代　大正期
図柄　色紙取り
唐織丸帯

P136-137

時代　昭和初期
生地　縮緬
図柄　落ち紅葉
技法　友禅
訪問着

P138-139

時代　大正期
図柄　有職幾何に鹿
唐織丸帯

P140-141

時代　明治期
生地　縮緬
図柄　横段染め
　　　源氏香に葵
子供着物

P142

時代　明治期
図柄　千代の冠と雅楽器
唐織丸帯

P143

時代　昭和中期
生地　綸子
図柄　鳳凰に桐と菊
技法　総刺繍
打掛け

P144

時代　大正期
図柄　雲取りに文庫
刺繍丸帯

P144-145

時代　昭和初期
図柄　船に胡蝶
刺繍綴れ帯

P146

時代　大正期
図柄　裂裟取りに
　　　　獅子と鳳凰
平織丸帯に刺繍

P146

時代　明治後期
図柄　松に飛鶴
唐織丸帯

P147

時代　大正期
図柄　東海道宿場図
刺繍昼夜帯

P147

時代　明治期
生地　綸子
図柄　光琳檜梅
技法　友禅
芸妓着物

P148

時代　大正期
図柄　百花繚乱に金鶏
染め丸帯に刺繍

P149

時代　大正期
図柄　万葉歌人の図
染め丸帯

P152-153

時代　昭和初期
生地　一越縮緬
図柄　立波に尾長鳥
技法　友禅
訪問着

P155

時代　明治期
生地　縮緬
技法　友禅
子供着物

P156

時代　昭和中期
生地　紋綸子
図柄　竹に桐
技法　絞りに刺繍
訪問着

P158-159

時代　昭和初期
生地　縮緬
図柄　八重桜に雉
技法　友禅
留袖

P160-161

時代　大正期
図柄　山茶花
羽織りを帯に
仕立て変え

P162-163

時代　昭和初期
生地　縮緬
図柄　菊桐に鳳凰
技法　友禅
振袖

P164-165

時代　大正期
生地　錦紗
図柄　縦縞に小菊
技法　友禅
重ね着物

P166-167

時代　大正期
生地　一越縮緬
図柄　霞暈し牡丹・
　　　菊扇
技法　友禅
振袖

P168

時代　昭和中期
図柄　色紙取り草花図
唐織袋帯

P168-169

時代　昭和中期
図柄　梅花と紅葉
染め名古屋帯

P169

時代　明治初期
生地　羽二重
図柄　地紙
技法　友禅
小振袖

P170

時代　昭和初期
生地　縮緬
図柄　桜に花
刺繍半襟

P171

時代　大正期
図柄　桜
唐織丸帯

P172-173

時代　昭和初期
生地　縮緬
図柄　犬筥
技法　型友禅
長襦袢

P173

時代　大正期
図柄　窓の景色
染め昼夜帯

P174-175

時代　大正期
図柄　酒呑童子
染め丸帯

P175

時代　大正期
図柄　紅葉と桜
染め昼夜帯

P176

時代　昭和中期
生地　銘仙
図柄　紫縞にモダン花
技法　織り

P177

時代　昭和初期
生地　縮緬
図柄　芙蓉
技法　型友禅
小紋

P180-181

時代　昭和初期
生地　お召し
図柄　光琳菊
技法　織り

P182-183

時代　昭和初期
生地　一越縮緬
図柄　モザイク菱に
　　　洋花
技法　友禅に刺繍
振袖

P185

時代　昭和中期
図柄　ダリヤ
絽綴袋帯

P186-187

時代　大正期
生地　紋綸子
図柄　矢羽絞りに
　　　薔薇刺繍
訪問着

P188-189

時代　昭和中期
図柄　栗の木
地描名古屋帯

P190

時代　大正期
図柄　桧扇
染め丸帯

P191

時代　昭和初期
生地　紋綸子
図柄　藤花下菖蒲池の
　　　対鯉
技法　友禅
振袖

P192

時代　大正期
図柄　アールデコ
昼夜帯

P193

時代　大正期
図柄　蝶に薔薇
両面帯

P194

時代　大正期
図柄　貝裄
唐織丸帯

P194-195

時代　大正期
図柄　桧扇に七宝
唐織丸帯

P195

時代　昭和中期
図柄　有職草花に小鳥
モール織袋帯

P198-199

時代　昭和初期
図柄　常盤松に紅葉
染め袋帯

P200

時代　昭和初期
図柄　流水に藤盛舟
刺繍名古屋帯

P203

時代　昭和初期
図柄　あやめ
刺繍りんず帯

P204-205

時代　大正期
図柄　雪持三蓋松
綴丸帯

P206-207

時代　昭和中期
生地　一越縮緬
図柄　風神雷神
技法　刺繍
黒留袖

P208-209

時代　大正期
生地　縮緬
図柄　楼閣山水に飛鶴
技法　友禅に刺繍
三枚重ね振袖

P210

時代　昭和中期
生地　緞子
図柄　観世水に飛鶴
技法　総刺繍
打掛け

P211

時代　明治期
生地　綸子
図柄　御所解
技法　友禅に刺繍
打掛け

P212

時代　昭和中期
生地　紋綸子
図柄　笹と桐に鳳凰
技法　総刺繍
打掛け

P213

時代　昭和初期
生地　縮緬
図柄　幔幕に菊と霞
技法　友禅
重ね振袖

P214-215

時代　昭和中期
図柄　花兎
唐織袋帯

P214-215

時代　昭和中期
図柄　カタバミ
紗袋帯

P215

時代　昭和中期
図柄　がく紫陽花
紗袋帯

P216

時代　昭和初期
生地　綸子
図柄　荒波
技法　友禅に刺繍
留袖

P217

時代　平成期
生地　紋織り
図柄　翔竜に雲
技法　地描
訪問着

P220

時代　昭和中期
図柄　源氏車に有職紋
唐織袋帯

P222-223

時代　大正期
図柄　片輪車
平織に刺繍袋帯

P224-225

時代　昭和中期
図柄　葵唐草
綾織丸帯

P225

時代　昭和初期
図柄　変わり亀甲に蝶
子供唐織丸帯

P226-227

時代　昭和初期
図柄　市松
子供平織丸帯

P226-227

時代　大正期
図柄　絞り矢羽に花
刺繍昼夜帯

P229

時代　昭和中期
生地　銘仙
図柄　花薬玉
技法　織り

弓岡勝美プロフィール

フリーのヘアー＆メイクアップアーティストとして活動していたのち現株式会社弓岡オフィスを設立、主宰となる。以後、雑誌、写真集やCDジャケット、CMなどの媒体を中心として活動する。又、着物の着付け・コーディネートなども手掛け、雑誌や写真集、CM、ドラマなどで活躍すると同時に着物のコレクションをはじめ、広告業界・雑誌業界・タレント業界向けに着物のレンタルを始める。

その後着物アンティークショップ「壱の蔵」を原宿に開く。以後、アンティーク着物ムーブメントの中心として精力的に活動を展開し、銀座松屋、横浜そごう、うめだ阪急などの百貨店催事にも参加。一方、古裂を使った押し絵やパッチワークなどの細工物も制作し展覧会を開催。その作風は上品で愛らしくファンも多い。主な著書『着物のお洒落自由自在 アンティーク着物』（世界文化社2002年）、『昔きもののレッスン12か月』（平凡社2003年）、『アンティーク振袖』（世界文化社2004年）、『きもの文様図鑑』（平凡社2005年）。

Katsumi Yumioka Profile

Yumioka started his career as a freelance hair and make-up artist. His work soon extended in to the world of magazine, CD cover jackets, TV Commercial and more. He also worked his way in to the world of Kimono styling, where he soon started collecting antique kimono.

Eventually, Yumioka's collection developed into his kimono antique shop, Ichinokura. Active as an instigator of the Japanese antique Kimono movement, he has vigorously expanded his work, including exhibitions held at the Ginza Matsuya, Yokohama Sogo, and Umeda Hankyu department stores. He is also famous for his patchwork designs using old Japanese cloth. He has published many Kimono books for the Japanese market.